Voltaire: A Very Short Introduction

Very Short Introductions available now:

Available soon:

For more information visit our website

www.oup.com/vsi/

Nicholas Cronk

VOLTAIRE

A Very Short Introduction

OXFORD
UNIVERSITY PRESS

Great Clarendon Street, Oxford, OX2 6DP,
United Kingdom

Oxford University Press is a department of the University of Oxford.
It furthers the University's objective of excellence in research, scholarship,
and education by publishing worldwide. Oxford is a registered trade mark of
Oxford University Press in the UK and in certain other countries

© Nicholas Cronk 2017

The moral rights of the author have been asserted

First edition published in 2017

Published in the United States of America by Oxford University Press
198 Madison Avenue, New York, NY 10016, United States of America

British Library Cataloguing in Publication Data
Data available

Library of Congress Control Number: 2016952560

ISBN 978-0-19-968835-7

Printed and bound by
CPI Group (UK) Ltd, Croydon, CR0 4YY

for Andrew

Contents

Voltaire

Acknowledgements

This book was begun during a fellowship at the Institut d'Études Avancées in Paris, and my warmest thanks go to its director Gretty Mirdal and to all her colleagues. For their comments and suggestions, I am enormously indebted to Alice Breathe, Lauren Clay, Andrew Curran, Paul Gibbard, Andrew Kahn, and Thomas Wynn. At the Press I wish especially to thank Andrea Keegan and Jenny Nugee for their unstinting help and encouragement.

List of illustrations

Voltaire

Introduction

I think that to not admire Voltaire is one of the many forms of stupidity.

(Borges)

Voltaire rarely leaves readers indifferent. He was a larger-than-life character, the greatest literary celebrity of the 18th century, and his fame was such that even now, 250 years later, it is hard to separate the individual from the 'image' he so assiduously cultivated. Over his long life of 84 years, he published extensively in almost every known literary genre, from verse to prose, from works of fantasy to works of political and religious polemic: the first full edition of his writings currently being undertaken in Oxford, and soon to be complete, will number around 200 volumes. He is a man of paradoxes: a 'modern' thinker, he revered the classics; he poured scorn on the genre of the novel, yet is remembered today primarily as the author of the satirical novel *Candide*. While Isaiah Berlin does not hesitate to call Voltaire 'the central figure of the Enlightenment', historians of ideas are often reticent in explaining precisely where his originality as a thinker resides.

Part of the problem lies in the ambiguity of the French term *philosophe*, which can designate both a philosopher, in the usual

English sense, and also a writer who popularizes ideas. The Italian Enlightenment thinker Pietro Verri puts his finger on the distinction when he says that 'Bayle [the 17th-century sceptic] convinced very few people; Rousseau, Voltaire, Diderot have ignited the spirits of many more. Readers want to be moved..., they must be shaken, and pushed towards the right path.' Voltaire was always good at shaking up received wisdom—'the best effect of a book', he wrote, 'is to make men think'—and his brilliance as a communicator and as a stylist might arguably be more significant than the originality of his thinking.

Voltaire's name has become firmly associated in the public mind with radical anticlericalism, so much so that the Victorian Oxford theologian Benjamin Jowett could write, a touch pompously, that 'civilization owes more to Voltaire than to all the Fathers of the Church put together'. This means that Voltaire has been, in France especially, a divisive figure, hated by pious Catholics as much as he has been idolized by free-thinking republicans. If the Enlightenment is defined as the 18th-century movement of ideas that ushered in ways of thinking that were not dependent on religion and on the individual's relationship to God, then Voltaire certainly occupies a central position in the emergence of modern secular society.

His unique career also tells us something important about Enlightenment culture more generally. What is interesting to us now is less the man baptized François-Marie Arouet than his alter ego, the author Voltaire who is his creation; and while it is hard to peer behind the mask, it is all too easy to fall into the trap of confusing man and mask. This book will therefore be an introduction to the making of an Enlightenment celebrity, an examination of the way Voltaire spent his whole life trying out different roles for size, perfecting various authorial postures, reinventing different ways to speak to and engage his audiences.

Theatre provides a powerful metaphor for how Voltaire created and sustained his life as a writer. He is perpetually conscious of being on stage, and his whole career can be viewed as an attempt to perfect this relationship with his audience. To admire Voltaire is to admire his performance.

Chapter 1
The man of theatre

Voltaire was, in all senses, a man of theatre. He wrote prolifically
for the stage—his fifty plays include comedies, tragedies, even
opera libretti—and it was as a writer of tragedy that he first, quite
literally, 'made' his name. François-Marie Arouet was born in Paris
in 1694, in either February (as he claimed) or November (as a
church baptismal record suggests)—everything concerning
Voltaire and religion is slippery. The youngest of five children, of
whom only three survived into adulthood, he was born into a
prosperous bourgeois family. His mother died when he was 7 and
at the age of 10, he was sent to the best school in Paris, the Jesuit
college Louis-le-Grand, where this son of a lawyer was educated
alongside members of the nobility, some of whom, like the future
marquis d'Argenson, would remain lifelong friends.

By all accounts an outstanding student, the young Arouet left
Louis-le-Grand at the age of 17 and started training as a lawyer. At
the same time, he frequented literary and poetic circles and began
to be known as a poet. His rejection of his father's attempts to
guide him into a career in the law was sealed in 1718 when he
invented a new name for himself. There are various theories about
the origins of 'Voltaire', one of the more plausible being that, as
both 'i' and 'j', and 'u' and 'v', are interchangeable in the Latin
alphabet, Voltaire can be read as an anagram of 'Arouet l[e] j[eune]'
('Arouet the younger'). Adding the particle 'de', usually a mark

of aristocracy, forms 'de Voltaire'—the new name amounting to an expression of social ambition and a desire for independence from his father.

Making a name

In the same year that he coined his new name, he enjoyed his first major literary success. Voltaire had begun work, probably as early as 1713, on a classical verse tragedy in the manner of the great 17th-century dramatists Corneille and Racine. The latter, for his first tragedy, had written *La Thébaïde*, dealing with the sons of Oedipus, and Voltaire decided to go one better, and chose for this first play the theme of Oedipus himself, a subject previously tackled by Corneille (1659), and before him by Sophocles and Seneca. For an unknown author to compete head-on with the greatest tragedians shows either extraordinary confidence or remarkable foolhardiness—and the young Voltaire showed signs of both. Nor is it necessary to be a Freudian analyst to wonder why a young man cutting off his links with his father and rejecting his father's name might be drawn to the classical myth of the Greek king who kills his father (and while Voltaire didn't marry his mother, he did end up in a marital relationship with his niece Marie-Louise).

For any writer who sought to establish himself in the *ancien régime*, the Comédie-Française, founded by a decree of Louis XIV in 1680, was the royal road to public recognition. It was here that Voltaire's first tragedy was produced in 1718, and it enjoyed a huge success. The Regent was present at the première, and the play had thirty performances in just its first run (new plays typically ran for fewer than ten performances), making it one of the major hits of the century. *Œdipe* is adroitly constructed. It pays deference to tradition in terms of its theme and structure and is composed in fluent verse, yet within this conventional framework, there are some surprises. Early audiences thought they could detect derogatory political allusions to the Regent, and there were certainly some references to religion which had a disconcertingly contemporary feel. Still only 24 years of age, Arouet became an instant literary star. *Œdipe* appeared in print the following year, in 1719, and the work's greatest piece of poetic invention appears in the signature on the title page: *Œdipe, tragédie, par Monsieur de Voltaire*.

For the rest of his life, wherever he found himself and whatever else he was writing, Voltaire would continue to write for the stage. He was a fluent writer of verse, and he was painstaking in trying to obtain the precise theatrical effect he required: he would send versions of his plays to his friends the comte and comtesse d'Argental for comment and criticism, and once a play had premièred, he paid careful attention to its reception, seeking to rewrite the scenes that had not been effective on stage: Voltaire, always, was highly attentive to the importance of performance. He was also attentive to theatrical fashion and to what pleased audiences, borrowing ideas from his fellow playwrights (and potential competitors) as necessary. He affected to despise the *opéra comique* (a musical genre in which accessible stories were told through song and spoken dialogue), yet he was more than happy for his stories to be staged as *opéras comiques*, as when Grétry used a libretto based on Voltaire's novel *L'Ingénu* (1767) for his first *opéra comique, Le Huron*, performed in Paris in 1768.

Reforming tragedy

Voltaire mistrusted *opéra comique* as a genre which had newly emerged in his own century, and he remained firmly wedded to the theatrical genres that in his view had reached a point of perfection in the reign of Louis XIV. Whereas some of his contemporaries, like Marivaux or Diderot, looked to imagine new theatrical forms, Voltaire remained true to the classical genres of the previous century. For him, Molière had set the standard for comedy, while Corneille and Racine had provided the models of verse classical tragedy. Voltaire, as his fame grew, would increasingly feel himself to be in competition with these predecessors, but while he sought tentatively to experiment with these classical models, he never sought to replace them—this posture of the radical who keeps one eye on tradition is typical of him. He adapted the classical model he had inherited, for example using a subject drawn from medieval history in *Tancrède* (1760), or introducing more striking scenic effects in *Sémiramis* (1749); and most daringly, he sought to update tragedy by introducing modern concerns, like religious toleration, in *Le Fanatisme ou Mahomet le prophète* (1741).

Zaïre (1732) provides a good example of his theatrical innovation. The action is set in Jerusalem at the time of the Crusades, and the heroine Zaïre, who was born to Christian parents but raised as a Muslim, is loved by the sultan Orosmane who becomes convinced that she has been unfaithful and stabs her. Voltaire's use of the theme of jealousy clearly owes much to Shakespeare's *Othello*, but whereas Shakespeare concentrates on the relationship between Othello and Iago, Voltaire focuses on the figure of Zaïre and her rediscovery of her brother Nérestan and father Lusignan. Although the basic structure—five acts, in alexandrine (twelve-syllable) verse—recalls the 17th-century classical tragedies of Corneille and Racine, Voltaire's approach to his subject matter is quite different. Rather than present some stark moral dilemma, he explores a range of softer emotions; and whereas classical dramatists had typically reworked subjects drawn from classical history and mythology, he here chooses a setting in more recent history that allows him to dramatize the contemporary preoccupation with religious difference. The play enjoyed huge success when it was first performed at the Comédie-Française, and it remained in the repertoire for the next two centuries, last being staged there in 1936.

Theatrical fame

A well-known painting of the Napoleonic era, Lemonnier's *Une soirée chez Mme Geoffrin* (1812), depicts a supposedly typical salon scene from the mid-1750s. Commissioned by Empress Josephine, it offers an entirely fictitious re-imagining of the Enlightenment Parisian salon of Mme Geoffrin. Gathered around the hostess are members of the aristocracy, like the duc de Richelieu, alongside the leading *philosophes* and intellectuals of the day, Buffon, D'Alembert, Montesquieu, Diderot, J.-J. Rousseau—and Voltaire, present in the form of a bust. At the centre of the picture, the most famous actor of the day, Lekain, is reading from Voltaire's tragedy *L'Orphelin de la Chine*, while those around gaze either at their hostess, or at the bust of Voltaire. The group has convened with the express purpose of listening to a Voltairean tragedy, so Voltaire manages to be at the centre of the proceedings without even being present.

Voltaire's plays appealed not just to actors and theatre-goers but to readers more generally. As he writes in a preface to one of his tragedies, *Adélaïde Du Guesclin*, 'when it comes to books, the readership numbers forty or fifty for serious works, four or five hundred for amusing works, and around eleven or twelve hundred in the case of a play'. In other words, he understood that printed plays were an effective means of reaching a wide audience, and he frequently published his own with prefaces and other prose texts, pieces that often extend or complement issues raised in the play, so that sometimes editions of his theatre come to resemble anthologies. Voltaire appears conventional in the way he follows the classical model of verse tragedy, but he is altogether unconventional in the way he publishes his plays to turn them into polemical works. His plays resonated far beyond the walls of the theatre, in France and across francophone Europe.

There is a rather oversimplified view that the 18th century marked 'the death of tragedy'; the genre of tragedy depended on certain shared religious beliefs, so the argument runs, and in the age of enlightened rationalism, it had lost its metaphysical foundation. Such a view fails to appreciate the enormous resonance of Voltaire's theatre in the 18th century; and overlooks too the extent to which that repertoire continued to hold audiences up until the first half of the 20th century. The great 18th-century English actor David Garrick is on record as saying that Voltaire was the greatest of the French tragedians, because he left space for the actor to embellish the text—a compliment indeed. Sarah Bernhardt (1844–1923), the dominant French actress of her age, was famous for her melodramatic death as Zaïre, a role which she first played at the Comédie-Française in 1874 and which she brought to London on her first visit in 1879. The Parisian photographer Étienne Carjat (1828–1906), a specialist in celebrity portraits, captured an image of Bernhardt in this role (see Figure 1): not only were Voltaire's tragedies performed well into the 20th century, they continued to serve as vehicles for the greatest star performers.

No Voltaire play has been performed at the Comédie-Française since *L'Orphelin de la Chine* in 1965, yet it would not be quite true to suggest that these tragedies have vanished entirely from the modern stage. Opera composers of the Romantic era sought out prestigious neoclassical sources for their libretti, and among the operatic versions of Voltairean tragedy are most famously Rossini's *Tancredi* and *Semiramide*, as well as Bellini's *Zaira* and later, Verdi's *Alzira*. The revival of interest in this bel canto repertoire since the 1960s, due in large part to remarkable coloratura singers such as Joan Sutherland and Marilyn Horne, has shown how Voltaire's tragedies, admittedly in a new musical guise, continue to hold audiences and provide starring roles for the leading artists.

The 18th century was stage-struck and Voltaire's plays appealed not just to theatre-goers in Paris, but all across France. The actor Lekain travelled in 1753 to Dijon, where in the course of a week, he performed in seven different tragedies, including Voltaire's *Œdipe* and *Mahomet*; he concluded the week in triumph, playing the role of Orosmane in *Zaïre*: 'There was such a crowd,' reported the local newspaper, 'that there has never been anything like it at the theatre.' The enthusiasm aroused by Voltaire's theatre was

1. Sarah Bernhardt in the role of Zaïre, 1874.

not confined to France. Troupes of French actors performed all across Europe in the 18th century and, in this cultural mission to 'civilize Europe', the theatre of Voltaire had a pre-eminent place. To take just the example of *Zaïre*, there were in the course of the 18th century translations into English, Italian, Dutch, German, Spanish, and Portuguese. In England, two translations were published, the second of which, *Zara*, an adaptation by Aaron Hill, enjoyed a major success at Drury Lane in 1736, when the title role was taken by the foremost English dramatic actress, Mrs Cibber; the play continued to be staged in England throughout the century by all the leading actors of the day, including Mrs Siddons (as Zara) and Garrick (as Lusignan), and the work was also performed in English in a number of cities in North America. In Russia, *Zaïre* was performed in French at a top academy for young cadets and later by women students at the first school for young women (modelled on France's Saint-Cyr), founded by Catherine the Great in 1764. Voltaire had become a modern European classic.

Voltaire as actor

Voltaire's exposure to the power of theatre began early, when he was a pupil at Louis-le-Grand. Acting played a central and crucial part in the curriculum of the Jesuits, who wrote plays for their pupils to perform and trained them in the nuances of performance. Theatre provided the ideal means of teaching classical rhetoric in action: how to construct arguments to make them most persuasive, how to convey emotions most effectively, how to project ideas by moving and instructing an audience with maximum effect—these are all lessons that Voltaire never forgot and that he applied in his writing far beyond his writing for the stage.

Voltaire must have acted when he was at Louis-le-Grand and he remained a keen actor—especially of his own plays—all through his life. So-called 'private theatres' were widespread in 18th-century

France among the bourgeoisie as well as the aristocracy and Voltaire himself built small private theatres, first at the château de Cirey and later at Ferney, where he created the Châtelaine theatre. Usually short of actors, Voltaire pressed everyone he could find into service and visitors were not spared: Louis Desmarets, who visited Cirey in 1739, wrote that in the space of forty-eight hours he was asked to perform in more than fifty acts from various plays. When Casanova visited Lausanne in 1760 (on his way to see Voltaire), he heard from ladies of the city who had acted with Voltaire in 'private' performances of his plays how brutally demanding the French author was, correcting them for the slightest error in pronouncing the verse and reprimanding one woman who in performing *Alzire* faked her weeping: 'He wanted us to shed real tears, and maintained that the actor could only make the spectator weep if he was truly weeping himself.'

In 1732, soon after the 'professional' première of *Zaïre*, Voltaire himself performed the role of Lusignan at the private theatre in the Parisian residence of Mme de Fontaine-Martel. The role of the noble patriarch who suffers imprisonment and exile while remaining true to his faith was clearly one that suited Voltaire and he went on performing it in other private theatres. It was still a favourite role over thirty years later, at Ferney, even if his acting was sometimes erratic—his secretary Wagnière recalls one performance in his memoirs:

> One day *Zaïre* was acted in his house, and he played Lusignan. At the moment of recognition of his daughter Zaïre, he burst into such a flood of tears that he forgot his part, and the prompter, who was also weeping, could not give him the reply. At this, he improvised on the spot half a dozen verses, entirely new and very good.

It is hard to know how much credence to give this anecdote—those close to Voltaire seem always to be willing collaborators in his myth-making. An English visitor to Ferney, Thomas Orde, saw him in this same role in 1772 and made a sketch from the life,

J.O. ft 1772

" Le Heros de Fernay au theatre de Chatelaine
"Ne proteur pas à trop, tu ne scaurais qu'écrire
"Tes Vers forcent. mes pleurs, mais tes gestes me font rire.
Anon.

2. Voltaire in the role of Lusignan (*Zaïre*), 1772.

showing the 78-year-old leaping about the stage, cutting an improbably comic figure in this tragic role (see Figure 2).

In the various recollections of Voltaire on stage, there is a recurring suggestion that he rather relished placing himself

13

at the heart of the spectacle. By all accounts his performances were filled with emotion, and he delivered his verses in grand oratorical style. Gibbon, who saw him perform in Lausanne, commented that 'his declamation was fashioned to the pomp and cadence of the old stage, and he expressed the enthusiasm of the poetry rather than the feeling of Nature'. He was clearly no method actor, but he certainly seems to have enjoyed playing roles with which he could identify—and in which he could be identified as Voltaire. Just as the role of Lusignan allowed him to portray the noble and persecuted patriarch, so he relished other roles that allowed him to project a version of himself: as Alvarez, in *Alzire*, he was an ageing leader defending a version of Christianity remarkably close to Voltairean deism; and as Argire, in *Tancrède*, he was the knight defending his daughter Aménaïde against an unjust death sentence, prefiguring the way that Voltaire would in the early 1760s defend the Huguenot Jean Calas. Voltaire was especially noted for his performance as Cicero, the great champion of liberty, in *Rome sauvée*, and Condorcet recalls in his posthumous biography of Voltaire the confusion created on stage between Voltaire the man and the person he was portraying:

> Never has any actor, in any role, carried illusion so far: we saw the Roman consul before our eyes. It was not verses recited from memory that we heard, but a speech flowing straight from the orator's soul. Those present at the performance over thirty years ago still remember the moment when the author of *Rome sauvée* cried out
>
> 'Romains, j'aime la gloire, et ne veux point m'en taire'
>
> [*Romans, I love glory, and will not deny it*]
>
> with such a ring of truth that one couldn't tell if this noble admission flowed from Cicero's soul, or from Voltaire's.

It has often been said that Voltaire inserted 'propaganda' into his tragedies by creating characters who were mouthpieces for his own views, but as we see here, the reality is more complex and theatrically more interesting. Blending Pirandello with Racine, Voltaire writes himself into his plays, creating characters who are, if not in search of their author, then performing variations of him. As in *commedia dell'arte*, characters adopt roles while remaining themselves—a device typical of comedy, but which Voltaire employs in tragedy, in the service of communicating serious ideas.

Voltaire's involvement in the world of theatre was total: he was an author and, as required, an actor, an impresario, a director, a prompter; even on the evenings when he came to the theatre simply as a spectator, he contrived to be part of the spectacle. As a young man, the story was told that he jumped onto the stage of the Comédie-Française during a performance of his tragedy *Artémire* (1720), in order to berate the audience. Fifty years later, he was still enjoying behaving badly at the Châtelaine theatre—the difference now, of course, was that the theatre was his. One British visitor to Ferney complained that Voltaire's 'frequent and outrageous interruptions' from the audience tended to detract from the action on stage, while another English visitor, John Moore, has left us with a memorable account of a performance at the Châtelaine theatre during which Voltaire, although not acting himself that evening, positioned himself so as to be seen by the entire audience (see Box 1). Visitors to Ferney clearly went to enjoy Voltaire's performance at the theatre—whether he was acting that day or not.

Voltaire's plays rank nowadays among his least familiar works. Yet if we wish to understand the extraordinary prestige he enjoyed in his own century and the influence he exercised, we cannot ignore his dominant presence in the theatre of his day. Theatre provided him with a powerful platform from which to speak, and he contrived to dominate the stage, all across Europe, for his entire literary career, lasting over half a century.

Box 1 A performance at the Châtelaine theatre at Ferney

I have been frequently at this theatre. The performers are moderately good. The admired Le Kain, who is now at Ferney, on a visit to Voltaire, sometimes exhibits; but when I go, my chief inducement is to see Voltaire, who generally attends when Le Kain acts, and when one of his own tragedies is to be represented.

He sits on the stage, and behind the scenes; but so as to be seen by a great part of the audience. He takes as much interest in the representation, as if his own character depended on the performance. He seems perfectly chagrined and disgusted when any of the actors commit a mistake; and when he thinks they perform well, never fails to make his approbation with all the violence of voice and gesture.

He enters into the feigned distresses of the piece with every symptom of real emotion, and even sheds tears with the profusion of a girl present for the first time at a tragedy.

I have sometimes sat near him during the whole entertainment, observing with astonishment such a degree of sensibility in a man of eighty. This great age, one would naturally believe, might have considerably blunted every sensation, particularly those occasioned by the fictitious distresses of the drama, to which he has been habituated from his youth.

The pieces represented having been wrote by himself, is another circumstance which, in my opinion, should naturally tend to prevent their effect on him. Some people indeed assert that this, so far from diminishing, is the real cause of all his sensibility; and they urge, as a proof of this assertion, that he attends the theatre only when some of his own pieces are to be acted.

> That he should be better pleased to see his own tragedies
> represented than any others, is natural; but I do not readily
> comprehend, how he can be more easily moved and deceived, by
> distresses which he himself invented. Yet this degree of
> deception seems necessary to make a man shed tears. While
> these tears are flowing, he must believe the woes he weeps are
> real: he must have been so far deceived by the cunning of the
> scene, as to have forgot that he was in a playhouse. The moment
> he recollects that the whole is fiction, his sympathy and tears
> must cease.
>
> (John Moore, an English visitor to Ferney, July 1772)

Caroline Lennox (Lady Holland) visited Ferney with her husband in 1767 and reported to her sister: 'I was at Voltaire's play, which entertained me of all things, tho' he did not act. The play was *Les Scythes*, a play of his own, and the *petite pièce*, *La Femme qui a raison*, his own also. They were really well acted, but the best part of the show was his eagerness and commendations both of the play and the performance.' The image that emerges from these anecdotes of the British visitors to Ferney is of Voltaire as master showman, as a performance artist always positioning himself in the limelight, and this image is key to our understanding of Voltaire as a writer more generally. As readers of *Candide* or of the *Traité sur la tolérance*, we find ourselves in precisely the same position as those friends invited to the intimate Châtelaine theatre: the performance moves and excites us, it may amuse us, it may sometimes make us weep, and throughout we are aware of Voltaire in the wings, pulling the strings, egging us on. The impresario enjoys puncturing the illusion as much as he enjoys creating it, and always he remains at the heart of the performance. More than a man of theatre, Voltaire is perhaps a master of theatrical performance, and this powerful sense of theatricality is central to all his literary performances.

Chapter 2
The Epicurean poet

Voltaire was a poet first and foremost, in his own eyes as well as in the eyes of his contemporaries, and throughout his long life he never stopped writing verse. The point needs to be emphasized because when we think of the great monuments of Enlightenment thought, like Diderot's *Encyclopedia* or Rousseau's *Social Contract*, we take it for granted that they are written in prose. Of course Voltaire also composed major works in prose, indeed he is regarded as one of the great prose stylists of the French language; but he wrote these alongside his numerous compositions in verse. The fact that he considered verse to be as good a vehicle as prose for expressing ideas makes him unique among the *philosophes*.

The quarrel about poetry

The Jesuit teachers at Louis-le-Grand instilled in Voltaire a deep and abiding love of the classics and of Latin literature in particular: all through his life he could quote Horace, Virgil, and Lucretius extensively from memory. Voltaire came to intellectual maturity in the early years of the 18th century when the learned world of Paris was riven by the Quarrel of the Ancients and Moderns. The party of the Ancients believed in the superiority of classical learning and wisdom, a position which would apparently seem to be one of cultural conservatism; whereas the Moderns wanted to argue that they could outstrip the achievements of the Ancient world and move beyond. Both positions were ideologically complex and could be identified with different cultural and political agendas, but in essence, this was an argument about the foundation of intellectual authority. Voltaire's response was characteristically paradoxical. On the one hand he had obvious sympathies with the Moderns' belief in progress and the advance of scientific understanding. Yet by cultural conviction, he was equally an Ancient who believed in the supremacy and continuing relevance of the classical models. The Moderns were notably hostile to verse, which they saw as an old-fashioned form of expression that needlessly complicated the clear and logical communication of ideas, and, in this respect, Voltaire aligned himself clearly with the Ancients who were staunch defenders of poetry.

An epic poem

There was no more powerful way to declare one's credentials as a poet than by writing an epic poem and that is what Voltaire set about doing when still in his late teens. The work that we know today as *La Henriade* was a highly ambitious project, begun around 1713. A number of epic poems had been written in France in the preceding centuries, but none had established itself in the canon, so Voltaire decided to write a national epic. He took as his subject the religious wars in France of the 16th century that were finally brought to an end when the Protestant Henry of Navarre converted to Catholicism to become Henry IV of France, thereby unifying the two warring parties. Voltaire's poetic model was Virgil and he introduced all the features familiar from classical epic, including the marvellous (such as the prediction of Henry IV's conversion) and allegorical figures such as Discord and Fanaticism.

At the same time, he gives his subject matter a modern political twist by making this poem an exemplification of the benefits of religious toleration. Perhaps rather naively, given the poem's evident criticism of the Catholic Church, Voltaire hoped for official authorization to publish in France and even asked that his work might be dedicated to the young Louis XV. The Regent, who knew Voltaire, swiftly declined the offer on the king's behalf and so Voltaire was obliged to produce a clandestine edition of his poem in Rouen in 1723, with the title *La Ligue* (the name of the party that defended Catholicism against the Protestants). He continued to revise and extend the poem, and the perfected version would be published in London in 1728, under the new title *La Henriade*, bearing a dedication to Queen Caroline. The work was acclaimed in Voltaire's lifetime and continued to be widely read and translated into the 19th century, by which time it had acquired classic status: Voltaire had achieved his aim of writing the national epic, he had become the Virgil of France.

Libertine verse

If writing an epic, even a controversial one, helped establish Voltaire as a serious poet, he cultivated in parallel what we can only call a semi-public face, writing libertine verses that circulated mainly in manuscript. Voltaire quickly gained a reputation as a poet of precocious fluency, and he was taken up by the Société du Temple, a free-thinking group including prominent aristocrats, which brought together some accomplished poets of the older generation, like Chaulieu and La Fare. They encouraged the young man, who imbibed from them the elegant libertine thinking that epitomized both their verse style and their lifestyle. The poetry cultivated at the Société du Temple was essentially light verse, dedicated to the Epicurean pleasures of wine, women, and song. Voltaire thrived in this atmosphere of iconoclastic liberty, and he showed a particular talent for satirical verses. Such poems circulated anonymously and rapidly made their author famous and infamous. The police were soon making copies of the 'anonymous' verses which they thought they could attribute to him, and poems making fun of the Regent landed Voltaire in trouble and the Bastille on more than one occasion.

The Epicureanism of this circle cannot however be reduced to the simple pursuit of pleasure. The Greek philosopher Epicurus taught that pleasure was the greatest good and was best achieved with the peace of mind that comes with modest living, freedom from pain and fear, and an understanding of the limits of one's desires. Pleasures of the mind were more important than physical pleasures, and the values of friendship were emphasized. Epicureanism was from early times regarded as a heresy by the Christian Church, but it regained greater visibility in France in the 17th century when the philosopher Pierre Gassendi translated and wrote a commentary on Book 10 of Diogenes Laertius, which deals with Epicurus. Voltaire would have known this work, and his Jesuit education had given him an intimate knowledge of the major expressions of Epicureanism found in the Roman poet Horace, whom he revered, and in Lucretius' poem *De rerum natura* (*On the Nature of Things*).

The metaphysical system of Epicureanism shaped Voltaire's thinking as much as its ethical principles. Epicurus held a materialistic view of the universe, according to which everything and everyone, including the gods, were made up of atoms. In this world-view, gods exist but there is no place for providence (the idea that the gods intervene in mankind's affairs with a purpose), so there is no need for prayer, and, disdaining religious superstition and fear of the gods, Epicureans reject all notions of an afterlife. Such a view can, but need not, lead to outright atheism. It has been said that Epicurus had 'a theology without a religion' and we might very well say the same of Voltaire. This belief in a god who created the universe but who thereafter kept his distance from men's affairs is generally referred to in the 18th century as 'deism' or 'natural religion' and such a notion clearly has its roots in Gassendi's revival of Epicureanism. Some scholars have questioned the 'sincerity' of Voltaire's belief in a deist god: the English Voltaire scholar Theodore Besterman was adamant that Voltaire was at heart an atheist, whereas a prominent French Voltaire scholar, René Pomeau, insisted, on the contrary, that

Voltaire's deism was a matter of genuine belief. To frame the question as a straight choice between atheism and deism is perhaps to adopt a modern rather than an 18th-century standpoint: Voltaire, always temperamentally inclined to practical solutions rather than to metaphysical speculation, was untroubled by the idea of (a) god who remained sensible and reasonable, like himself.

What is beyond argument is that Voltaire's religious beliefs, such as they are, have their sources in classical—pre-Christian—thought, and that his knowledge of Epicurus came not from reading the prose works of the philosophers but primarily from the magnificent verse of the Epicurean poets Horace and Lucretius in the original Latin. Nothing more natural, then, than that he should use verse to write about religion, and the work that really established his credentials as an ironist critical of religious orthodoxy was a poem, his *Épître à Uranie*. In this anonymous poem, the poet adopts the persona of a 'latter-day Lucretius', explaining the mysteries of religion to an imagined mistress. He suggests that the Christian God is cruel and has made us in his image; he denounces Christian doctrine while admiring Jesus' ethical teachings; and he concludes with a defence of 'natural religion' and of a god whom all mankind knows to be just. Voltaire composed this manifesto in 1722, perfectly aware that his bold indictment of Christianity was unprintable. But publication did not have to be in print: under the law of the *ancien régime*, manuscripts were not subject to the same system of censorship as printed books, so Voltaire circulated his *Épître à Uranie* anonymously in manuscript. When challenged, he coolly replied that the poem had been written by his revered mentor, the abbé de Chaulieu—a fiction that suited everyone as by that date Chaulieu was conveniently dead.

Voltaire would continue writing poetry until his dying breath and, while not all his poetry can be described as Epicurean, the philosophical inspiration of his early years remains a constant theme. The libertine vein of Epicureanism finds ample expression in *La Pucelle*, a bawdy mock epic poem about Joan of Arc, which Voltaire circulated in manuscript to his close friends—the subject matter made an authorized publication impossible. As Bernard Shaw remarked in the preface to his play *Saint Joan* (1923), the poem aimed 'to kill with ridicule everything that Voltaire righteously hated in the institutions and the fashions of his own day'. Voltaire also contributed to the contemporary debate about luxury with a poem, *Le Mondain* (1736). Again, the inspiration is Epicurean—the poem is memorable, among other things, for the image of the popping champagne cork as an emblem of modernity—but the philosophical debate is serious, and the poem is in part a defence of the use of verse for the discussion of ideas. In a fine late work, the *Épître à Horace* (1772), Voltaire contrasts his lot with that of the Roman poet: whereas Horace had to accommodate Augustus, Voltaire has no obligation to pay homage to monarchs. The notion of serious philosophical verse was becoming outdated by the 1770s—yet at the age of 78, Voltaire was still keen to present himself in poetic dialogue with the greatest Epicurean poet of them all.

Stances à Mme Du Châtelet

This poem typifies Voltaire's lyric voice at its most persuasive. The *Stances à Mme Du Châtelet* were composed in 1741, when Voltaire was in his late forties:

> Si vous voulez que j'aime encore,
> Rendez-moi l'âge des amours.
> Au crépuscule de mes jours
> Rejoignez, s'il se peut, l'aurore.
>
> Des beaux lieux, où le dieu du vin
> Avec l'amour tient son empire,
> Le temps qui me prend par la main,
> M'avertit que je me retire.
>
> De son inflexible rigueur
> Tirons au moins quelque avantage.

Qui n'a pas l'esprit de son âge,
De son âge a tout le malheur.

Laissons à la belle jeunesse
Ses folâtres emportements;
Nous ne vivons que deux moments,
Qu'il en soit un pour la sagesse.

Quoi! pour toujours vous me fuyez,
Tendresse, illusion, folie,
Dons du ciel qui me consoliez
Des amertumes de la vie.

On meurt deux fois, je le vois bien;
Cesser d'aimer et d'être aimable
C'est une mort insupportable,
Cesser de vivre, ce n'est rien.

Ainsi je déplorais la perte
Des erreurs de mes premiers ans,
Et mon âme aux désirs ouverte
Regrettait ses égarements.

Du ciel alors daignant descendre,
L'amitié vint à mon secours;
Elle était peut-être aussi tendre,
Mais moins vive que les amours.

Touché de sa beauté nouvelle,
Et de sa lumière éclairé,
Je la suivis, mais je pleurai
De ne pouvoir plus suivre qu'elle.

In his remarkable translation, the modern American poet Richard
Wilbur skilfully reproduces the formal shape of Voltaire's verse,
including his octosyllabic lines:

If you would have my heart love on,
Grant me such years as suit the lover,

And teach my twilight to recover
(If but it could) the flush of dawn.

Time takes my elbow now, in sign
That I must bow and turn away
From gardens where the god of wine
Divides with Love his pleasant sway.

Let us from rigorous Time obtain
What timely blessings may assuage.
Whoever will not be his age
Knows nothing of his age but pain.

Leave then to sweet and giddy youth
Those ecstasies which youth can give:
Two moments only do we live;
Let there be one for sober truth.

What! Will you leave me thus forlorn,
O tenderness, illusion, folly—
Heavenly gifts whereby I've borne
Life's bitterness and melancholy?

Two deaths we suffer. To forgo
Loving, and being loved in turn,
Is deathly pain, as now I learn.
Ceasing to live is no such woe.

Thus did I mourn the loss of all
Those years when I was young and mad,
My slow heart sighing to recall
The furious beat which once it had.

Friendship, descending from above,
Came then in mercy to my aid;
She was as kind, perhaps, as Love,
But not so ardent, and more staid.

Touched by her charms, so fresh they were,
And by her radiance calm and clear,
I followed her; yet shed a tear
That I could follow none but her.

Wilbur's version beautifully captures Voltaire's elegiac tone, as the poet laments the passing of time and the loss of youth, and resigns himself to the fact that friendship has come to replace love. There is little new in the sentiments expressed, which is perhaps why it is hard to argue for Voltaire as having an original poetic voice; but the musicality of the verse and the fluent elegance with which he revisits these traditional Epicurean themes are hugely appealing and have made this poem justly celebrated. Voltaire creates a remarkable intimacy with his reader, and it seems he first composed the poem as part of a letter. In July 1741 he was staying in Brussels with his companion Émilie Du Châtelet, and he included these verses in a letter to his old school friend Cideville, a magistrate in Rouen and a lover of poetry. The seemingly hackneyed opposition between love and friendship acquires new potency in this context, as Voltaire, in the company of his mistress, writes to his oldest friend. Given the apparent intimacy of the verses, it seems fitting that Voltaire did not rush to publish them—but then, he did not need to. Copies were made and passed around, and within two years the poem found its way into print in a journal; from 1746 the piece was included in collections of Voltaire's writings. The mystique of this poem, that it was an essentially private communication that had somehow strayed into print, was what ensured its success.

And its success was huge. The poem was frequently reprinted and the composer La Borde, who knew Voltaire, set it to music. In the 19th century, the lyric was acclaimed by the Romantic writer Chateaubriand and translated into Russian by Alexander Pushkin. Poets continue to respond to these verses and Ezra Pound produced an imitation of the poem, 'making it new' by recreating it in the style of Imagism (see Box 2). Pound responded to Voltaire's verses while also being wholly receptive to what Voltaire stood for as a philosopher: he approved of Voltaire's robust rationalism and translated the article on the Book of Genesis from the *Dictionnaire philosophique portatif*, because, as he wrote to Margaret Anderson in April 1918, 'a reminder that "There was once a man called Voltaire" can do no harm'.

Box 2 Ezra Pound: To Madame du Châtelet

If you'd have me go on loving you
Give me back the time of the thing.

Will you give me dawn light at evening?
Time has driven me out from the fine plaisounces,
The parks with the swards all over dew,
And grass going glassy with the light on it,
The green stretches where love is and the grapes
Hang in yellow-white and dark clusters ready for pressing.

And if now we can't fit with our time of life
There is not much but its evil left us.

Life gives us two minutes, two seasons—
            One to be dull in;
Two deaths—and to stop loving and being lovable,
That is the real death,
The other is little beside it.

Crying after the follies gone by me,
Quiet talking is all that is left us—
Gentle talking, not like the first talking, less lively;
And to follow after friendship, as they call it,
Weeping that we can follow naught else.

The Ancient versus the Modern

Voltaire's strategy for becoming recognized as a writer is clear.
Precociously talented as a poet and supremely confident of his
abilities, he set out with deliberation to establish himself in the
poetic genres of classical tragedy and epic poetry, acknowledged
since Aristotle as the most prestigious and the most challenging.
At the same time, not content with merely imitating the classical
tradition, he was determined to innovate too. Voltaire acquires
from the libertine tradition of the previous century not only a
poetic style but a way of thinking, and his Epicureanism is

inherited from this poetic tradition. According to this Epicurean world-view, man is a sentient being and the starting-point of all philosophical reflection. Voltaire is rational in his approach to problems and deeply hostile to anything that smacks of the metaphysical. Belief in human reason, dislike of dogma, openness to doubt: these are his watchwords and they are already present in the early works of the Epicurean poet.

An abiding preoccupation with religion underlies the broad range of Voltaire's early works. In the *Épître à Uranie* he speaks openly of 'natural religion' as a set of beliefs shared by all humanity (and broadly consistent with the ethical values of the New Testament): 'Remember that the eternal wisdom on high has engraved with his own hand natural religion in the depths of your heart.' In *La Henriade*, we read the line 'God engraves in all hearts the law of nature': the tone is slightly more sober, less overtly didactic, as befits an epic poem, but the idea is the same. Even in a classical tragedy like *Œdipe*, we come across sly allusions to the innocence of men facing cruel gods, or attacks on priests as impostors.

Voltaire is conservative in his choice of classical models, but innovative in his use of them: his solution is to be Modern by being an Ancient. From the beginning, he acquired the reputation of being a free-thinker and a thorn in the side of the authorities, a reputation he was never to lose. At the same time, he sought, if not respectability, at least recognition. This tension between wanting simultaneously to be an insider and an outsider is wholly characteristic of him, and it is a tension that is lifelong. In so many ways, Voltaire is the nostalgic radical, the conservative iconoclast.

Voltaire is now remembered above all for his antagonism to Christianity and to established religion generally, and he established this reputation early on, through the medium of poetry. Two things are striking about his early incarnation as an Epicurean poet. First, his extraordinary and precocious talent.

And secondly, his rashness and lack of caution. He early
established a reputation for reckless comment, but in 1726,
he experienced a serious setback when a nobleman whom he had
ridiculed had him publicly beaten by his servants (the chevalier
de Rohan, it seems, directed operations from the safe distance of
his carriage). The idea that poets were fit to be beaten (in French,
à rouer—one reason he had had to ditch the name Arouet) was
a cliché, and what greater humiliation for a poet than to become a
cliché? Voltaire's pride was wounded beyond repair, and his
humiliation would have important consequences.

Chapter 3
The Englishman

During the French election campaign of 2007, presidential candidate Nicolas Sarkozy came to London and surprised his audience of French businessmen working in the City by telling them that they were following in the footsteps of Voltaire.

> As trade enriched the citizens of England, so it contributed to their freedom, and this freedom on the other side extended their commerce, whence arose the grandeur of the state.

These words, which would not have been out of place in Sarkozy's Anglophile speech, come from Voltaire's *Letters Concerning the English Nation*, first published in London in 1733. The myth that Voltaire came to England as an exile, fleeing the tyranny of the Bastille for a land of liberty, is well known. It makes for a good story, all the more so as Voltaire helped write it, but it is essentially a myth. The truth, more prosaic but no less interesting, is that he came to London on a business trip. He was keen to publish a definitive edition of his epic *La Henriade*, and as censorship made this impossible in France, he resolved to oversee the production of an edition in London. It was while he was organizing the letters of introduction he would need in England that disaster struck. Following his humiliating public beating, the hot-headed Voltaire had to be interned in the Bastille to prevent him from challenging Rohan to a duel and he was finally released on condition that he leave immediately for England. His imprisonment delayed his journey to England; it was not the cause of it.

His choice of destination is not surprising: the Revocation of the Edict of Nantes in 1685 had removed from French Protestants, known as Huguenots, the limited protection offered them by Henry IV, and as a result many left France to settle in the Low Countries or England. Among the Huguenots who settled in London there were a number who worked in the print trade, so in the 1720s there was a community of French-speaking printers and publishers, working in an area to the north of what is now the Strand, all of them highly skilled and more than willing to publish works in French that might annoy the Catholic kingdom of France.

Voltaire learns English

Voltaire arrived in London in May 1726 and went to stay with his friend, the merchant Everard Fawkener, who lived in Wandsworth, then a country village to the south of the city. He had little or no English and immediately began taking lessons from a young Quaker, who many years later published an account of how he taught Voltaire English using Addison's *Spectator*. By the time the London 'season' began later in the year, Voltaire was in the city, and from 1727 to 1728, he lodged at the White Peruke in Maiden Lane (a green plaque at the back of the Vaudeville Theatre now marks the spot), conveniently close to the French-speaking printers of the capital. Other 18th-century French writers visited England—Montesquieu, Prévost, Jean-Jacques Rousseau—but they were visitors and no more. Voltaire's journey was different, both on account of the length of his stay (he was to remain nearly two-and-a-half years, leaving in the autumn of 1728), and because he worked hard to achieve fluency in English.

Voltaire immersed himself in this new culture and was soon reading widely in English. He went frequently to the theatre in London, in particular to see performances of Shakespeare, and he quickly made the acquaintance of the leading writers and poets of the day. His name was already known in England, but it is clear that his networking skills were phenomenal. He got to know John Gay, who showed him the text of *The Beggar's Opera* before it had been performed, and also Jonathan Swift, whose *Gulliver's Travels* he read as soon as they were published, in 1727. Voltaire clearly made an impact with his newly acquired English: Alexander Pope invited him to supper at Twickenham, and the story goes that when Pope's elderly mother inquired solicitously about Voltaire's poor health, he replied: 'Those damned Jesuits, when I was a boy, buggered me to such a degree that I shall never get over it as long as I live.' Thomas Gray, to whom we are indebted for this anecdote, adds disapprovingly that 'this was said in English aloud before the servants'. Another story in circulation was that the French poet had ridiculed Milton's allegorical treatment of Sin and Death in *Paradise Lost* (a poem which he otherwise admired), and this led Edward Young to compose an epigram for Voltaire:

> You are so witty, profligate, and thin,
> At once we think thee Milton, death, and sin.

There is little evidence that Voltaire took much interest in the visual arts or in opera, which enjoyed much prestige in London at this time, thanks to Handel. Voltaire was a man of words and what interested him was English literature. A letter has recently come to light which Voltaire wrote to the first Earl Bathurst, a Tory grandee and prominent opponent of Walpole's administration, and a sophisticated literary patron who included among his friends such writers as Pope, Swift, Prior, Congreve, and (later) Sterne. It is a thank-you letter, written from Paris in 1729, in impressively fluent English, soon after Voltaire's return from England, and delivered by Stephen Fox (later Lord Ilchester):

> My Lord, I hope the sense of my gratitude for all the kindnesses
> your Lordship showed me when I was at London, will be more
> acceptable to you if it passes through Mr Fox's hands. I'll never
> forget as long as I live your lordship's favours to me, the amiableness
> of your character, the freedom of your house, the many liberties
> I enjoyed in that charming library at Richings...

It is striking that Voltaire recalls enjoying 'the freedom of [the] house' of one of England's greatest literary patrons, and that he relished the liberty of having access to the great house's library. Voltaire was no typical tourist: he came to England to learn and to publish, and he achieved his goals by adroitly building new social networks.

Voltaire and the London world of publishing

Voltaire wrote a short book in English about epic poetry and the history of the French civil wars, and it appeared in London, in December 1727, under the title *An Essay Upon the Civil Wars of France and also Upon the Epic Poetry of the European Nations from Homer down to Milton*. This was in effect a marketing exercise, designed to prepare the English reading public for *La Henriade*, due to appear a few months later, and Voltaire does not hesitate to address the English reading public in English:

> It has the appearance of too great a presumption in a traveller, who
> hath been but eighteen months in England to attempt to write in a
> language, which he cannot pronounce at all, and which he hardly
> understands in conversation...I look upon the English language as
> a learned one, which deserves to be the object of our application in
> France, as the French tongue is thought a kind of accomplishment
> in England. Besides, I did not learn English for my private
> satisfaction and improvement only, but out of a kind of duty.

Three months later, in March 1728, the epic poem *La Henriade* was published in London, a handsome quarto edition priced at three guineas, beautifully printed with fine copperplate engravings. The text is in French, but the dedication, in large capitals, is in English: 'To the Queen'—Queen Caroline, who as Princess of Wales had granted the impoverished French poet a pension. Voltaire financed the publication of this edition by enlisting subscriptions, and the list of subscribers included in the volume is a roll-call of the leading families of the kingdom, both Whig and Tory: we can only marvel at Voltaire's social networking skills. He had accomplished the task he had set himself in coming to England and he might now have returned to France. But he had a new project in mind, which he had already alluded to in the introduction to his *Essay Upon the Civil Wars of France*:

> I am ordered to give an account of my journey into England … I
> will leave to others the care of describing with accuracy, Paul's
> church, the Monument, Westminster, Stonehenge, etc. I consider
> England in another view; it strikes my eyes as it is the land which
> hath produced a Newton, a Locke, a Tillotson, a Milton, a Boyle,
> and many great men either dead or alive, whose glory in war,
> in state affairs, or in letters, will not be confined to the bounds of
> this island.

In other words, Voltaire announces his intention to write an account of his journey to England. The travel account was a well-worn literary genre and visitors to England had ritually to pass judgement on the beauty of the women or describe a trip to Oxford. But as is clear from his programmatic statement here, Voltaire was no typical tourist, and if he did go to Oxford, we have been spared his probably caustic comments on what he found there. His project was not to write a conventional travel book but to do something new: to produce a portrait of a nation by describing the 'great men' of literature and learning.

The *Letters on the English*

Voltaire began writing his *Letters on the English* in England in 1727 and continued to work on the book after his return to France. He wrote the book in French, but the first edition to appear was an English translation, *Letters Concerning the English Nation*, in London in 1733; a French edition followed in London, and a slightly extended version in French appeared the following year in France, under the title *Lettres philosophiques*. The work is made up of twenty-odd short essays, grouped thematically and dealing with religion, politics, science, and literature. Together they constitute the portrait of a culture and what is, in effect, a manifesto of Enlightenment values. The style is witty and concise, the tone familiar and often ironical, and the work presents English culture in a favourable but sometimes ambiguous light. Here, for example, is how Voltaire introduces the Church of England:

> England is properly the country of sectarists: *In my father's house are many mansions*. An Englishman, as one to whom liberty is natural, may go to heaven in his own way.

> Nevertheless, though everyone is permitted to serve God in whatever mode or fashion he thinks proper, yet their true religion, that in which a man makes his fortune, is the sect of Episcoparians or Churchmen, called the Church of England, or simply the Church, by way of eminence. No person can possess an employment either in England or Ireland, unless he be rank'd among the faithful, that is, professes himself a member of the Church of England. This reason (which carries mathematical evidence with it) has converted such numbers of dissenters of all persuasions, that not a twentieth part of the nation is out of the pale of the established church. The English clergy have retained a great number of the Romish ceremonies, and especially that of receiving, with a most scrupulous attention, their tithes. They also have the pious ambition to aim at superiority.

Clearly at one level this is a plea for religious toleration: the Englishman 'may go to heaven in his own way', whereas in France only one religion is tolerated by the state. But irony, which is so much Voltaire's stock in trade, has a happy habit of complicating arguments and how we read this passage depends very much on which side of the Channel we imagine ourselves. The English reader of the time would doubtless have been amused by the satire of the established Church and its preoccupation with power and wealth; the French reader, with no special knowledge of the English Church, would have been likely to interpret this passage metaphorically as a description of the power-hungry Jesuits in France and to read the satire accordingly. Voltaire is writing about England, but not only England.

Voltaire's *Letters on the English* are often read as being as much about France as about England: his praise of the English is understood as an indirect strategy for criticizing their neighbours across the Channel. There is obviously some truth in this, but Voltaire's voice can rarely be taken at face value. The French reader would of course understand praise of English religious tolerance as an implicit critique of French persecution of the Huguenots. But what would English readers, and especially English Catholics, have made of Voltaire's account that all in England lived 'happy and in peace'? The Test (1673) and Corporation (1661) Acts discriminated against Catholics and Dissenters, making them liable for higher taxation and limiting their civil rights—Catholics were banned from teaching and from attending a university, they were not entitled to vote, to hold public office, or to own property. Posing as the well-meaning foreign commentator, Voltaire rather plays down this discrimination against English Catholics and trots out the usual clichés about English liberty. English readers might well have found irony in this calculated equivocation: you talk a lot about your liberties, he seems to be saying to the English, but perhaps you're not as tolerant as you think you are. Voltaire's *Letters on the English*, published in both English and French, in both England and

France, is a book aimed at both countries. Voltaire, in other words, writes deliberately with different audiences in mind. And that desire to create a dialogue, or even multiple dialogues, is of course a typical Enlightenment strategy: dialogue erodes certainty and favours tolerance.

The message about religious toleration, central to this work, is aimed at the whole of Europe. One of the *Letters on the English* describes the Royal Exchange, an imposing building in Cornhill, in the heart of the City, rebuilt after the Great Fire, where merchants from across the world met to transact business (not to be confused with the Stock Exchange, a later creation). The example of the Exchange as a place of cultural transfer had already been used by Addison in a well-known essay in *The Spectator*, and Voltaire here quite deliberately responds to Addison, introducing a new dimension, which is religion. While religious differences separate men, it is trade, Voltaire suggests, that brings them together:

> Take a view of the Royal Exchange in London, a place more venerable than many courts of justice, where the representatives of all nations meet for the benefit of mankind. There the Jew, the Mahometan and the Christian transact together as though they all professed the same religion, and give the name of infidel to none but bankrupts. There the Presbyterian confides in the Anabaptist, and the Churchman depends on the Quaker's word. At the breaking up of this pacific and free assembly, some withdraw to the synagogue, and others to take a glass. This man goes and is baptised in a great tub, in the name of the Father, Son and Holy Ghost: that man has his son's foreskin cut off, whilst a set of Hebrew words (quite unintelligible to him) are mumbled over his child. Others retire to their churches, and there wait for the inspiration of heaven with their hats on, and all are satisfied.

> If one religion only were allowed in England, the government would very possibly become arbitrary; if there were but two, the people would cut one another's throats; but as there are such a multitude, they all live happy and in peace.

The Royal Exchange was one of the capital's iconic modern buildings and Voltaire starts here with what we expect to be a touristic description ('Take a view of...'). But immediately he turns the Exchange into a metaphor, to demonstrate how political freedom, religious freedom, and international trade are all mutually dependent and reinforcing. Questions of commerce had not really been part of political theory before the 18th century and, as István Hont has argued, it is only in Voltaire's lifetime that success in international trade becomes crucial to the military and political survival of nations. This seemingly innocent description of the Royal Exchange is a bold political statement therefore, and one all the more radical for being expressed in a deceptively simple and witty voice.

The *Letters on the English* also contain a series of 'letters' or short essays dealing with science and philosophy, and it is these accounts of Bacon, Locke, and Newton that caused the greatest controversy in France when the book was published. Newtonian physics was poorly understood but controversial in France, where Newton's views were contrasted unfavourably with those of Descartes. This subject matter might seem somewhat arid, but Voltaire is a master at popularizing complex ideas. So he introduces the difference between Cartesian and Newtonian physics as if it was simply one more touristic experience:

> A Frenchman who arrives in London will find philosophy, like everything else, very much changed there. He had left the world a plenum, and now he finds it a vacuum. At Paris, the universe is seen, composed of vortices of subtile matter; but nothing like it is seen in London. In France, 'tis the pressure of the moon that causes the tides; but in England 'tis the sea that gravitates towards the moon...

Ask any schoolchild today what they know about Newton and they'll tell you about the apple falling on his head: the story is firmly established as a piece of popular mythology. And the survival of this anecdote is due very largely to Voltaire. He heard it apparently from Newton's niece and immediately understood that this simple homely image was the perfect way of expressing the pleasing simplicity of Newton's explanation of the force of gravity. Voltaire used the story first in his *Essay on Epic Poetry* in 1727, then again in his *Letters on the English*, and the story took root, never to be forgotten: Voltaire has left his mark on English popular culture.

In presenting the thought of Locke and Newton, Voltaire is keen to drive home the importance of empiricism and the experimental method, which he contrasts with the deductive Cartesian approach, rooted in the notion of innate ideas. In the interests of producing a telling and simple dichotomy therefore, he ignores the empirical tradition that also existed in France, for example with the philosopher Gassendi. We should avoid relying on inherited superstition, Voltaire says, and we must be open to persuasion by the facts. His journalistic feel for the telling anecdote comes into play again, when he tells the story of how the English came to embrace the practice of inoculation:

> In the beginning of the reign of King George I, the Lady Wortley Montague, a woman of as fine a genius, and endued with as great a strength of mind as any of her sex in the British kingdoms, being with her husband who was ambassador at the Port, made no scruple to communicate the smallpox to an infant of which she was delivered in Constantinople. The chaplain represented to his lady, but to no purpose, that this was an unchristian operation, and therefore that it could succeed with none but infidels. However, it had the most happy effect upon the son of the Lady Wortley Montague, who, at her return to England, communicated the experiment to the Princess of Wales, now Queen of England...

> The moment this Princess heard of inoculation, she caused an experiment of it to be made on four criminals sentenced to die, and by that means preserved their lives doubly; for she not only saved

them from the gallows, but by means of this artificial smallpox, prevented their ever having that distemper in a natural way...

The Princess being assured of the usefulness of this operation, caused her own children to be inoculated. A great part of the kingdom followed her example, and since that time ten thousand children at least of persons of condition owe in this manner their lives to Her Majesty, and to the Lady Wortley Montague; and as many of the fair sex are obliged to them for their beauty.

This account is interesting first of all for the importance it attributes to two influential women. Their pragmatic rejection of superstitious practices shows that empiricism is really nothing more than womanly common sense. Voltaire sets up a rather simplistic antithesis between the innate ideas of Descartes and the empirical approach of Locke. But behind this opposition, what interests him is less the science than the broader application of these ideas. Cartesian innate ideas are associated with religious authoritarianism and with the divine rights of absolutist kings; empiricism, on the other hand, is associated in English culture with the Whig political settlement in which the power of the king is constrained, and a pragmatic religious consensus whereby a state Church tolerates other beliefs, within certain limits. So science matters, not least, because it underpins a religious and political ideology.

Voltaire: Anglophile and Englishman

The Bloomsbury Group author Lytton Strachey, with just a touch of bombast, wrote that 'the visit of Voltaire to England marks a turning point in the history of civilisation'. It is certainly true that Voltaire's encounter with English culture had far-reaching consequences for him and for the Enlightenment generally. For the rest of his life, Voltaire was marked as an Anglophile, the man who made the name of Shakespeare known throughout Europe—Oliver Goldsmith, in his (delightfully unreliable) *Memoirs of M. de Voltaire*, paints a vivid picture of Voltaire defending the English against French prejudice in a Parisian salon (see Box 3).

Box 3 Voltaire defends the English in a Parisian salon

As a companion no man ever exceeded Voltaire when he pleased to lead the conversation, which however was not always the case. In company which he either disliked or despised, few could be more reserved than he; but when he was warmed in discourse, and had got over a hesitating manner which sometimes he was subject to, it was rapture to hear him. His meagre visage seemed insensibly to gather beauty, every muscle in it had meaning, and his eye beamed with unusual brightness. The person who writes this memoir, who had the honour and the pleasure of being his acquaintance, remembers to have seen him in a select company of wits of both sexes at Paris, when the subject happened to turn upon English taste and learning. Fontenelle, who was of the party, and who being unacquainted with the language or authors of the country he undertook to condemn, with a spirit truly vulgar began to revile both. Diderot, who liked the English, and knew something of their literary pretensions, attempted to vindicate their poetry and learning, but with unequal abilities. The company quickly perceived that Fontenelle was superior in the dispute, and were surprised at the silence which Voltaire had preserved all the former part of the night, particularly as the conversation happened to turn upon one of his favourite topics. Fontenelle continued his triumph till about twelve o'clock, when Voltaire appeared at last roused from his reverie. His whole frame seemed animated. He began his defence with the utmost elegance mixed with spirit, and now and then let fall the finest strokes of raillery upon his antagonist; and his harangue lasted til three in the morning. I must confess, that, whether from national partiality, or from the elegant sensibility of his manner, I was never so much charmed, nor did I ever remember so absolute a victory as he gained in this dispute.

(Oliver Goldsmith, *Memoirs of M. de Voltaire*, 1761)

The *Letters on the English* are a masterpiece, a succinct and punchy political manifesto masquerading as a travel account, that helped to shape the way the Enlightenment saw itself. Religious dogmatism was harmful and offensive to human reason and, worse than that, it was bad for business. Exchange of ideas went hand in hand with exchange of material goods, and freedom in both was liberating. Locke and Newton could be pressed into service to show that an empirical, open-minded approach to problems was always superior to dogmatism and led to better government and a happier society. Other thinkers in the 18th century, like Diderot and d'Holbach, were exploring atheistic materialism, but Voltaire remained wary of this development: critical of established religion certainly, he was firmly opposed to atheism and keen to retain some minimal notion of the divinity, for reasons pragmatic rather than metaphysical. His presentation of Locke and Newton in the *Letters on the English* is designed to bolster this compromise notion of deism. Along with the English language, Voltaire has learned English pragmatism. His reforming English voice is, in the final resort, a voice of moderate radicalism, but it is also a persuasive narrative and a call to action.

Whether Lytton Strachey is correct in arguing that Voltaire's visit to England was so decisive is a moot point. In fact, Voltaire knew a certain amount about England before he set foot in the country: in the early 1720s he had been in frequent touch with Lord Bolingbroke, the prominent Tory politician and writer then living in exile at La Source (near Orléans), through whom he learned about a wide range of English writers; Shakespeare, for example, was already beginning to be discussed in France at this time. Similarly, the core thesis of the *Letters on the English*, namely that freedom of religious belief and freedom of trade go hand in hand, is one that he had already formulated in connection with the Low Countries, which he had visited before coming to England; indeed much that Voltaire says about England had already been said in the late 17th century by Sir William Temple, about the United Provinces.

Even so, the *Letters on the English* constitute a major turning point in Voltaire's evolution as a writer and thinker. We saw how his earlier writings were marked by Epicureanism, and those same, broadly deist, ideas—the basic belief in god, but mistrust of any form of metaphysics—continue to underlie this new work. There was an active current of deist debate in early 18th-century England, involving such figures as John Toland, Anthony Collins, Matthew Tindal, and Thomas Woolston, and it was once fashionable to argue that they influenced Voltaire's thinking. 'Voltaire's early philosophical deism was strengthened and modified by the deistic disciples of Locke', writes Norman Torrey, adding that 'in his later attack against the Christian religion [Voltaire] adopted every method that was used by his English predecessors'. It is perhaps surprising, then, that these thinkers are nowhere discussed in the *Letters on the English*—Voltaire is more interested in poking fun at the Quakers, whose dress and manners provide rich material for amusing anecdotes, but whose fundamental beliefs concerning the place of God in the world coincide substantially with his own.

What is new in the *Letters on the English* is that Voltaire has now found modern thinkers who can be pressed into service in support of his Epicurean-inspired world-view. Whereas before he had relied essentially on Latin literature (Horace, Cicero, Lucretius) to think about religion, now he rests his argument on modern English thinkers (Bacon, Locke, Newton). Moreover, his religious views, in the context of these English thinkers, now expand into a broader political and economic model of progressive, enlightened thinking.

Furthermore the *Letters on the English* mark a highly significant moment in Voltaire's career: his emergence as a great prose-writer. Until now he had been seen as a poet, and it is only in England, confronted by new styles of prose-writing such as Addison's *Spectator*, that he finds his voice in prose. It is a remarkable and instantly recognizable voice, concise, ironical, often cheeky. This is far removed from the high-flown and, to modern ears, rather pompous prose that was typical of both English and French writing in the late 17th century. It is no criticism to suggest that the *Letters on the English* are in some ways a work of brilliant journalism: the personal and witty style draws in the reader, while the work is divided into short, easy-to-assimilate chunks, and complex ideas are summed up in attractive images, like the apple to explain Newton's law of gravity. Addison and his friend Steele are often regarded as the founders of modern English prose, forging a form of language, the 'middle style' as Dr Johnson called it, that was clear and easy, and spoke comfortably to a wide range of readers. Voltaire similarly revolutionizes French prose, bringing the acerbic wit that is his trademark and forging a new language capable of expressing and communicating fresh ideas.

Voltaire

In the end it is Voltaire's encounter with the English language that is the most decisive aspect of his visit to Britain. After only a few months in the country, he wrote to his friend Thieriot that England was a country where he could 'learn to think', and in April 1728, he informed a French friend (in English) that 'I think and write like a free Englishman.' Voltaire had acquired an English voice and was trying it out for size. For a period, he seems to have flirted with the notion of settling permanently in England, of becoming an honorary Englishman, but that plan came to nothing. Even so, the pose of the free-thinking Englishman would stay with him all his life. Once back in France, he wrote to a friend (in French), 'If you had spent two years in England as I did, I am sure that you would have been so touched by the energy of the language that you would have written something in English.' Forty-odd years later, when he was living in the château de Ferney, he regaled his British visitors with his outbursts of English: 'When he talked our language he was animated with the soul of a Briton', declared James Boswell, who was also impressed by Voltaire's command of imprecations: 'He

swore bloodily, as was the fashion when he was in England.'
Voltaire flattered another group of British visitors with a
remarkable oath: 'If ever I smell of a resurrection, or come
a second time on earth, I will pray God to make me be born in
England, the land of liberty.'

Chapter 4
The scientist

One of Voltaire's lesser-known claims to fame is that he was a Fellow of the Royal Society. He was elected in 1743, three years before his elevation to the Académie française, and this public recognition was important to him. When he wrote to the President of the Royal Society, the noted atheist Martin Folkes, accepting his fellowship, he went to lengths to remind him of his Anglophile credentials:

> One of my strongest desires was to be naturalized in England; the Royal Society, prompted by you vouchsafes to honour me with the best letters of naturalization. My first masters in your free and learned country were Shakespeare, Addison, Dryden, Pope. I made some steps afterwards in the temple of philosophy towards the altar of Newton. I was even so bold as to introduce into France some of his discoveries; but I was not only a confessor to his faith, I became a martyr.

When Voltaire wrote this, it had been fifteen years since he had left England and, as we see, he had lost none of his fluency in English, and none of his propensity to self-dramatization.

The reference to his becoming 'a martyr' is an allusion to the furore that followed the publication of the *Lettres philosophiques*

in France: in May 1734, a *lettre de cachet* was issued against
Voltaire, rendering him liable to arrest, and on 10 June the
Paris *parlement* (a court of law rather than a parliament)
issued a decree declaring that his work was 'scandalous,
contrary to religion, good morals and the respect due to
authority', and ordering that a copy of the *Lettres philosophiques*
be ceremoniously burned in the courtyard of the *parlement*.
All this put Voltaire in an extraordinarily delicate position.
On the one hand, the provocation and irritation he caused the
authorities was as ever a keen source of pleasure to him, and,
in retrospect, we can say that he had found his distinctive voice
as a prose-writer. On the other hand, it was not clear how he
could now capitalize on this *succès de scandale*. Even once the
danger of a humiliating imprisonment had passed, he had to
work out what to do next. In the 18th century, as in the 21st,
French cultural life was centred on the capital, but Voltaire was
no longer welcome in Paris or Versailles. So the problem facing
him was twofold: what, in future, should he speak about? And
from what platform should he speak? The two questions can
never be easily separated when discussing Voltaire.

A curious insight into Voltaire's career at this moment is
provided by the portrait that Quentin de La Tour painted in
1735. The original oil is lost, but several copies survive
(including one at the château de Versailles), and the portrait
reached a wide audience through the medium of print and as a
frontispiece to many Voltaire editions (see Figure 3). La Tour
was on the brink of establishing himself as a portraitist at this
date (he would show his portraits in the Salon from 1737), so he
was not as famous as his sitter, and the portrait undoubtedly
served both their careers. It depicts Voltaire in half profile, in a
dignified pose, and in the original painting holding a book. No
hint here of the dramas and dangers connected with the *Lettres
philosophiques*: this is the established writer, calmly
authoritative, that in 1735 Voltaire yearned to be.

MARIE FRANCOIS AROUET DE VOLTAIRE

Voltaire

POST GENTIS HIC CARUS ERIT,
NUNC CARUS AMICIS

3. Engraving by Nicolas Jean Baptiste Poilly after the 1735 portrait of Voltaire by Quentin de La Tour.

The château de Cirey

Voltaire had recently met and fallen in love with Émilie Du Châtelet, a woman of aristocratic breeding and formidable intellect. She was determined to pursue her studies, and she too had a problem. If it was difficult for Voltaire to know how to position himself as a writer after the scandal of the *Lettres philosophiques*, Du Châtelet faced a different difficulty: as a woman, she had virtually no model for imagining any public life as a writer, scientist, and intellectual. Laura Bassi, who taught Newtonian physics at the University of Bologna and who was a correspondent of Voltaire's, was only just making her reputation as a woman scientist during these years. Voltaire and Du Châtelet were passionately in love and had two big advantages in facing the world together: her social standing, which to some extent protected them from public opinion, and her considerable wealth, which included several properties, including a rather dilapidated château at Cirey in north-eastern France, on the borders of the Champagne region. So the decision was taken, with the agreement of Du Châtelet's obliging husband, that she and Voltaire would leave Paris and move to the relative isolation of Cirey and there pursue their studies and their writing: this was a way of turning exile into a studious paradise and it would last, with inevitable interruptions, for some fifteen years, from 1734 until Du Châtelet's death in 1749. Each occupied separate luxuriously appointed apartments, and their friends were equally admiring of the luxury and of the fierce regime of work which they observed: visitors to the château were told not to leave their rooms before ten in the morning, so that Voltaire and Du Châtelet could work undisturbed.

The years spent at Cirey were remarkably productive for them both. Voltaire continued to write plays and poems, as he had always done, and in prose he began to work on several historical works as well as to experiment tentatively with short stories. He even installed a tiny theatre under the eaves—it can still be visited today—where he and his guests could perform for each other. But the most remarkable change was that he set out to reinvent himself as a scientist. He had returned from England with an intellectual framework clearly in place: Locke and Newton were the cornerstones of an empirical world-view, according to which the philosopher discovers truth through experiment. Now Voltaire set out to become an empirical philosopher and to be taken seriously as a writer on scientific matters, and he began to work to deepen his understanding of Newtonian physics.

The Newton wars

There was keen debate in the first half of the 18th century about theories of planetary motion. French thinkers, like Fontenelle and Dortous de Mairan, defended the theory of Descartes, according to which space was filled with matter, and fluid vortices determined the movement of planets. The Englishman Newton proposed something different: for him, the universe consisted of empty space, and all heavenly bodies moved through this empty space subject to the force of gravitational attraction. The first French scientist to contrast the two systems of Descartes and Newton was Maupertuis, who published his *Discours sur les différentes figures des astres* in 1732, just in time to influence Voltaire who was then putting the finishing touches to his *Letters on the English*. So in the autumn of 1732, Voltaire began a correspondence with Maupertuis, inviting him to explain certain aspects of Newtonian theory: 'Your first letter baptised me in the Newtonian religion,' he wrote to him, 'with your second I received confirmation. Thank you for administering the sacraments'—Maupertuis may have proved the better scientist in the long run, but Voltaire was always the funnier writer. Then in May 1733, Voltaire met Émilie Du Châtelet, who had previously taken Maupertuis as her mathematics tutor, then as her lover (prefiguring Cunégonde, who in the first chapter of *Candide* enjoys with her tutor a lesson in 'natural philosophy'). Having taken Maupertuis's place as Du Châtelet's lover, Voltaire resolved to learn more about science too.

Through the 1730s and 1740s, Maupertuis, Voltaire, and Du Châtelet would defend the Newtonian position against the Cartesians, in what J. B. Shank has called the 'Newton Wars'. From our modern perspective, Newtonianism is closely linked to the rise of the Enlightenment, but the notion that Newton simply ousted Descartes because his ideas were superior is too simplistic. The 'Newton Wars' were to a large extent an institutional battle, in which the (pro-Newton) young turks took on the (pro-Descartes) establishment. Voltaire's decisive move at an early stage to ally himself with Maupertuis may have been because he was intellectually persuaded by the superiority of Newtonianism, or it may also have been motivated by his strategic desire to be seen as a challenger to conventional ways of thinking.

Émilie Du Châtelet was Voltaire's most powerful ally in his desire to deepen his understanding of science. The old idea that she was the modest handmaiden to Voltaire's genius is now well and truly discredited, and the recent discovery of some of her scientific manuscripts only confirms her status as a significant scholar in her own right and certainly a far greater scientific mind than Voltaire. Her *Institutions de physique*, published in 1740 and long underestimated as a mere introductory textbook, is now understood to be a serious attempt to reconcile the positions of Leibniz and Newton. Her most important and enduring achievement was to translate Newton's *Principia* from Latin into French, and her version, completed in 1749, the year of her death, remains today the standard French translation of this work.

Du Châtelet provided him with every material comfort and support, and a new one-storey wing was built in which Voltaire housed his library and laboratory. Many items of scientific equipment were ordered from Paris, and in 1737 Voltaire even engaged a chemist to act as his assistant: he was setting himself up as an experimental scientist. Françoise de Graffigny, a writer who came to stay in late 1738, recalled that as they sat at dinner in

Voltaire's gallery, she could see the globes and scientific instruments that he used for his experimental research.

Voltaire clearly learned much from Émilie Du Châtelet and wrote two works designed to promote her views and work; she was an important, even at times a competing, influence on his own intellectual development. When the Académie des sciences announced the topic for the essay competition of 1738 as the nature of fire, Voltaire decided to enter; so too did Du Châtelet, who submitted her essay without informing her companion. Once it emerged that neither had won, Voltaire magnanimously arranged for both their submissions to be published alongside the three prize-winning essays. In other areas they clearly disagreed, for example on the subject of *vis viva* ('live force'), an argument in 18th-century science about why a body in motion will keep moving until stopped by an obstacle or the effect of friction. Voltaire wrote an essay on the subject, *Doutes sur la mesure des forces motrices et sur leur nature*, which was presented to the Académie des sciences and published in 1741; what is notable about his attempted solution to the problem is his firm opposition to the philosophical ideas of Leibniz and Wolff, in effect a silent refutation of the opinions of Du Châtelet.

Voltaire's most important scientific work to emerge in this period is his *Éléments de la philosophie de Newton*, an extensive account of Newtonian physics, which appeared in 1738. This work used to be routinely dismissed as a work of 'mere' vulgarization, but that is to severely underestimate Voltaire's achievement. The book gives extended accounts of Newton's ideas on optics and on gravitational theory, and it immediately provoked a number of responses, ranging from pamphlets to a 400-page book by the Cartesian physicist Jean Banières. Voltaire published a full reply, which in due course provoked a further response, in 1739, from two other physicists: Voltaire had started a debate. He continued to make revisions to the *Éléments*, adding in 1741 an entire first part dealing with the implications of Newtonian theory for arguments concerning the existence of God—a text he had hesitated to include previously and that he had published separately, in 1740, under the title *Métaphysique de Newton*. The *Éléments de la philosophie de Newton* had long-lasting impact, and between 1738 and 1785 it went through no fewer than twenty-six editions; the work played a key role in spreading knowledge of Newton in Europe and also in re-establishing and re-orienting Voltaire's reputation. It was certainly on account of the *Éléments* that he was elected to the Royal Society. Voltaire remained blissfully unaware of Newton's extensive writings on alchemy and religion, which came to light much later and which would not at all have suited the view of Enlightenment that Voltaire was so painstakingly constructing.

Voltaire the sceptic

In the 1760s and 1770s, Voltaire returned to scientific concerns, notably engaging in contemporary debates about biology and geology, for example in *Les Singularités de la nature* (1768). His name would always attract readers—this last work provoked a response in England, *Remarks on M. de V********'s New Discoveries in Natural History* (Bath, 1770). But in truth these discussions of biology and geology—'natural philosophy' in the language of the period—are works of polemic more than of science. Voltaire, concerned with the effect of these debates on the argument for a deist supreme being, is not persuaded that they are methodologically sound. As William Barber remarks:

> These whole areas of enquiry concerning the nature and history of living things, and the history of the earth itself, were thus in Voltaire's time largely fields for speculative controversy based on what now seem non-scientific premises, rather than firmly founded branches of human knowledge. And for Voltaire the contrast with the solid achievement of Newtonian physics was clearly an acute one.

In his account of Newtonian physics, Voltaire insists on Newton's wisdom in not adventuring into areas that are uncertain, like the immortality of the soul: 'He knew how to doubt.' Perhaps the long-term lesson he takes away from Newton is scepticism, and even if, in later years, his interests move away from experimental science, he always insisted on the importance of understanding 'the limits of human understanding'—this is the title of an article in his *Dictionnaire philosophique* (1764). Voltaire's scepticism, on questions of religion for example, is not just the consequence of a pragmatic accommodation with the authorities; it is central to his philosophical world-view, and he likes to quote Montaigne's dictum 'Que sais-je?' ('What do I know?'). He does not believe that metaphysics should have a role in scientific debate and his *Métaphysique de Newton*—in effect a reply to Du Châtelet's *Institutions de physique*—celebrates Newton as a philosopher who avoided unnecessary metaphysical speculation. This continues to be the central plank of a much later work, *Le Philosophe ignorant*, published in 1766. Composed as a series of fragmentary 'doubts', this work reiterates the absurdity of various metaphysical systems in order to underline the foolishness of religious superstition and the necessity of doubt as a first step towards achieving religious toleration and social justice.

Voltaire and the academies

We no longer think of Voltaire as a scientific writer and his works in this area are largely forgotten. To some extent, the story of Voltaire setting out to become an experimental scientist is a story of failure, but it's a failure that tells us much about the man and about the way he was trying to shape his intellectual development and his position as a public figure. His commitment to empiricism and his practical desire to become an empirical researcher are immensely revealing. Voltaire felt himself a Newtonian at heart, a man who clearly preferred physics to metaphysics. Moreover he was on the right side of history: when the *Éléments* were first published, Cartesian views still dominated the Académie des sciences, but by the mid-century, Newtonian views had come to the fore. In his *Discours préliminaire* (1751), the philosophical and methodological preface to the *Encyclopédie*, D'Alembert hails Locke and Newton as the forerunners of modern progressive, empirical thinking; this is the Voltaire line and it had become—and still largely remains today—the standard narrative of the Enlightenment.

Voltaire remained a controversial and therefore vulnerable writer however, and he felt severely the lack of institutional approbation. In 1743, Dortous de Mairan stepped down as perpetual secretary of the Paris Académie des sciences and Voltaire let it be known that he would like to succeed him. This important and influential post, previously held by Fontenelle, would have given him a position of status in the capital. D'Alembert had just been elected to the Académie des sciences in 1741, so the Cartesian party was beginning to lose its dominance and Voltaire seemed a credible candidate. But his reputation was too risky. According to the astronomer Jérôme Lalande, it was an offhand remark that put Voltaire out of contention: when asked what attracted him about Versailles, Voltaire is supposed to have replied, 'it is not the master of the house'. The choice of successor fell on the less distinguished but infinitely safer Jean-Paul Grandjean de Fouchy.

Having failed in his bid to join the Académie des sciences, his election in the same year to the Royal Society in London must have come as especially welcome news. Voltaire valued the prestige of association with academies and in 1746 he wrote an essay in Italian contesting the theories of Buffon, *Saggio intorno ai cambiamenti avvenuti sul globo della terra* (*Essay on the Changes that have Happened to the Earth*), as a reception for the Academy of Bologna; he was subsequently elected to several other Italian academies, on the basis of the same work. Meanwhile, he had long had his eye on the Académie française, where his candidacy had been mooted as early as 1731. He was a candidate in 1742 and again the following year, but failed on both occasions, in large part because memories of the controversy surrounding the *Letters on the English* had still not faded. Finally Voltaire managed to placate his enemies at court and on his third attempt, in 1746, he was elected to the Académie française. He was now one of the forty 'immortals' and his career, it seemed, would be made in the French capital.

Chapter 5
The courtier

Voltaire had a keen sense of the pragmatic necessity of finding an
accommodation with power. He worked hard throughout his life
to establish and defend his status as an author within the social
hierarchy of the *ancien régime*, with varying degrees of success but
with unflagging determination. The French Revolution would
turn Voltaire into a hero who had valiantly struggled against the
ancien régime, but nothing could be further from the truth.
A confirmed monarchist, Voltaire could never quite understand
why he found monarchs so hard to get along with.

Aristocratic connections

Voltaire was socially ambitious and not just for reasons of
simple snobbery: he understood that social position was
essential to grounding his voice and position as a writer. When
he decided to adopt the name Voltaire, he didn't merely give
himself a *nom de plume*, he ennobled himself at the same time:
'Monsieur de Voltaire' was a significant social promotion from the
bourgeois 'Monsieur Arouet'. Voltaire may not have known the
acid put-down of the Versailles courtier and memoirist, the duc
de Saint-Simon—'Voltaire's father [a lawyer] worked for my
father'—but he knew well the aristocratic condescension that lay
behind it. Following the death of Louis XIV in 1715, Voltaire
did his best to impress the Regent, the duc d'Orléans, but his

need for approval was always at odds with his need to provoke, and he could not restrain himself from circulating satirical verses about the Regent which quickly landed him in trouble. From the start, Voltaire had a challenging relationship with authority.

Throughout his life, Voltaire counted many nobles among his friends and his strategic cultivation of these aristocratic friendships was crucial in defending himself against criticism and attack (both real and imagined). He corresponded with the duc de Richelieu, a man of great influence at court, over a period of more than half a century and their letters suggest a genuine friendship; however friendship did not preclude lobbying, quite the contrary. And so, in between flattering references to the duke's military and sexual prowess, for example, Voltaire will slip in an admiring reference to his preferred candidate for the next vacancy at the Académie française. He took great care to nurture his friendship with the comte and comtesse d'Argental, whom he always addressed as 'mes chers anges' (my dear angels)—he meant, of course, guardian angels—writing long letters to them over many years about literature and especially theatre. The publication of *Candide* provides a good example of how Voltaire exploited his aristocratic connections. The novel was published in early 1759, but the year before, Voltaire sent the work, in instalments, to the duc de La Vallière and this manuscript (rediscovered in the Arsenal Library in Paris in the 1950s) remains the only manuscript of the novel known to us. Voltaire sent it to La Vallière ostensibly to ask for his advice (and he did take note of some of his suggestions), but it is hard not to think that he also had an ulterior motive: knowing that the book was likely to cause a rumpus, it did no harm to have a manuscript copy in the safe keeping of a duke well placed at Versailles. Voltaire used relationships such as these over many years to help secure his reputation at court, but what he most aspired to was to be at court himself and to occupy a position of influence.

Voltaire at the French court (1725, 1745–6)

The first major portrait that we have of Voltaire is by the court painter Largillière and dates from the years 1724–5. Writers were typically portrayed holding a pen or seated at a writing desk, but this is quite different, as Largillière depicts the 30-year-old Voltaire dressed in his court finery, staring confidently at the viewer. In 1725, the court gathered at Fontainebleau to celebrate Louis XV's marriage to Marie Leszczynska, daughter of Stanislaw, the deposed king of Poland. This was an affair of state and Voltaire was present for the celebrations, striving to please the new queen by reading her his plays: 'I was very well received here by the Queen,' he wrote to his friend Thieriot. 'She wept at *Mariamne*, she laughed at *L'Indiscret*, she speaks often to me, she calls me my poor Voltaire.' In other letters from this time, Voltaire complains about the obligations of court life, and this early attempt to gain the king's favour came to nothing. In 1726, Voltaire became embroiled in scandal and he left for England soon after.

Voltaire's second chance came in 1745. He had then been in quasi-exile at Cirey for over a decade and he was anxious to re-establish himself in the capital. The Dauphin Louis was to marry Maria Theresa Raffaela, the Infanta of Spain, an alliance of obvious dynastic significance for the Bourbons, and great celebrations were planned. As part of the court festivities, Voltaire was invited to the court, where his first duty was to furnish the libretto of a three-act musical work, *La Princesse de Navarre*, to be set to music by Rameau. There had been no celebrations on this scale since the reign of Louis XIV, and the work, first performed at Versailles in February 1745, enjoyed considerable success. The choice of genre for the new work, a *comédie-ballet*, is significant: this courtly genre, mixing theatre and dance, had been prominent in the 1660s and 1670s, when Molière had collaborated with Lully (*Le Bourgeois gentilhomme*) and latterly with Charpentier

(*Le Malade imaginaire*). Stepping into the shoes of France's greatest playwright Molière, the courtier Voltaire belatedly basks in the warmth of the Sun King's reign.

In April 1745, Voltaire was appointed *historiographe de France*: the post of Royal Historiographer had existed intermittently since the Middle Ages and carried ill-defined duties but undoubted prestige. Voltaire was enjoying a winning streak, and the following month, in May, the maréchal de Saxe led French troops to a notable (and rare) victory against the English-led coalition at the Battle of Fontenoy (part of the ongoing War of the Austrian Succession). It was a good time to be Royal Historiographer, especially as the king of France had been present in person on the battlefield, and Voltaire's remarkable fluency as a poet stood him in good stead: his celebratory *Poème de Fontenoy* was completed in record time and rapidly printed by the royal presses.

In November 1745, Voltaire and Rameau collaborated again, this time on an opera to celebrate the monarch himself. *Le Temple de la gloire* was premièred at Versailles in the theatre specially constructed that year in the Grande Écurie, and included all the greatest singers of the day, including Marie Fel and Pierre Jélyotte. After two performances at court, it was performed at the Opéra in the city of Paris in December 1745 and was revived there in a revised version the following year. This is an opera about the nature of true kingship. After a prologue including a famous monologue sung by the personification of Envy (a nod to Quinault, Lully's librettist in the previous century), two kings, Bélus, who is too tyrannical, and Bacchus, who is too pleasure-loving, are successively expelled from the temple of glory. Finally it is Trajan who is crowned with laurel by Glory and, having gained victory over the two rebel kings, he shows clemency and pardons them in a climactic scene of sublime reconciliation. Too modest to accept the glory on his own account, Trajan finally asks the gods to transform the temple of glory into a temple of happiness for the people.

It was a tricky business to write a celebratory opera that would please the king and court, and Voltaire's libretto for *Le Temple de la gloire* is enormously skilful—and encouraged Rameau to write glorious music. Whatever Voltaire touches, he is always trying to gently modernize and here he is attempting to reform the genre of opera, replacing the traditional vapid love interest with more serious moral content, reducing the amount of recitative, and introducing more stage spectacle. When the work was revived in 1746, Voltaire's reforms were watered down and, although the libretto remained in print, the music was lost. The score of the revised 1746 version was published in 1909 by Saint-Saëns, while the music of the 1745 version, the one truest to Voltaire's intentions, has only just turned up in the university library at Berkeley: Voltaire's greatest operatic achievement can only now be fully appreciated.

In April 1746, Voltaire was finally elected to the Académie française. In a sense, this was an honour long overdue: his fame and brilliance as a writer were not in dispute, but his election was an official sign that he was now also deemed 'acceptable' as a writer. This was the recognition he had long sought and, in December 1746, the king allowed Voltaire to purchase the post of Gentleman of the King's Bedchamber (*gentilhomme ordinaire de la Chambre du Roi*): the holders of this position numbered around forty and were mostly aristocrats; they performed small diplomatic tasks for the king and had automatic access to his chamber, so enjoyed the privilege of an official apartment at Versailles when they were present at court. The position came with significant tax breaks, but above all, for someone like Voltaire, it provided access to people of influence.

But in the end it couldn't work. Voltaire did not possess the temperament of a courtier and Louis XV knew it. The honeymoon of 1745 and 1746 was bound to end in tears and it did, with a tawdry incident at the queen's gaming tables, when

Émilie Du Châtelet lost all her money and Voltaire was overheard making a remark to the effect that she was playing with crooks. The couple had to leave Versailles immediately, no doubt to the relief of all. When, in 1749, Voltaire decided to accept Frederick's invitation to attend his court at Potsdam, he was obliged to renounce his title of Royal Historiographer; he also sold on his charge of Gentleman of the Bedchamber, but by special dispensation he was allowed to keep the title and the honours and duties that went with it. His performance as a Versailles courtier had been short-lived, but for the rest of his life he would continue to sign formal letters with the title *gentilhomme ordinaire de la Chambre du Roi* (see Figure 4).

Nous ferons long-temps fous & infenfibles au bien public. On fait de tems en tems quelques efforts & on s'en laffe le lendemain. La conftance, le nombre d'hommes néceffaire & l'argent manquent pour tous les grands établiffemens. Chacun vit pour foi. *Sauve qui peut* eft la dévife de chaque particulier. Plus les hommes font ihattentifs à leur plus grand intérêt, plus vos idées patriotiques m'ont infpiré d'eftime. J'ai l'honneur d'être, &c.

Voltaire , gentilhomme ordinaire de la chambre du roi.

Au château de Ferney, par Geneve, ce 22 avril 1768.

4. A letter published in the *Mercure de France*, July 1768: Voltaire signs with his full court title, *gentilhomme ordinaire de la chambre du roi* ('Gentleman of the King's bedchamber').

Voltaire, Frederick, and Catherine

In England in the late 1720s, Voltaire had frequented members of the English court and made the acquaintance of the princess of Wales, soon to become Queen Caroline and the dedicatee of *La Henriade*. In 1736, Voltaire began his lifelong correspondence with Frederick of Prussia, then crown prince, and the two men met for the first time in 1740. After he became king, Frederick repeatedly invited Voltaire to join him in Potsdam and, although clearly tempted by the invitation, Voltaire had to decline as long as he was living with Émilie Du Châtelet—the marquise did not share his enthusiasm for the young Prussian king. The immediate result of her death in 1749 was that Voltaire was able at last to accept Frederick's long-standing invitation and he arrived at the Prussian court in Potsdam in 1750. He did not become a German in Berlin in the way that he had become an Englishman in London—as he rarely left the French-speaking court, he had little need to learn German. He harboured the ambition of becoming a privileged adviser to Frederick, intellectual counsellor to a Philosopher King, but this idyll soon soured. Frederick was a man of the Enlightenment in his private views, but a hard-nosed pragmatist in matters of state. Voltaire angered the king when he began a savage war of words with Maupertuis, the President of the Prussian Academy of Sciences, and his position eventually became untenable. His departure from Berlin in 1753 turned into a public humiliation, when he was in effect roughed up by soldiers in Frankfurt as he left German territory. Henceforth Voltaire would live on his own terms, away from the courts of Europe. But his cultivation of enlightened despots did not end there. Later in life Voltaire entered into an extensive, much publicized, correspondence with Catherine the Great. She entreated him to visit her in Russia with as much urgency as he pleaded his desire to meet her, each outdoing the other in epistolary insincerity. They never met in person and so they never argued: but their epistolary exchanges are a two-handed literary masterpiece.

Belatedly, Voltaire had learned his lesson as a courtier: flatter with the written word—and keep your distance.

Voltaire as court historian

Voltaire's numerous works of history are no longer widely read, but in his lifetime, they counted, together with his theatre and poetry, among his major claims to fame. His historical masterpiece is perhaps his *Siècle de Louis XIV*, which he began writing in the 1730s at Cirey and would finally publish in Berlin in 1751. This is a portrait of the Sun King and his age, and Voltaire's experience as a courtier at Versailles was formative: as Royal Historiographer, he had access to precious archives; as a courtier he could observe at first hand the politics and intrigues of court life.

Despite his well-advertised claims that he intended to portray French culture of the 17th century in its entirety, much space is devoted to military affairs and Louis XIV's many successes in battle—Voltaire cannot escape traditional military history as easily as he thinks. But he also discusses other aspects of the culture, in particular devoting long chapters to the importance of religion, where he is on difficult ground. Louis XIV was famous for his belief in 'un roi, une loi, une foi' ('one king, one law, one faith'), whereas Voltaire clearly believes that religious toleration is a prerequisite for a polite and commercial society—that had been one of the major lessons of the *Letters on the English*. In the *Siècle*, he downplays his critique of the religious policies of Louis XIV, for he needs to balance criticism of this aspect of the king's reign with praise for his actions elsewhere. This is a delicate balancing act, for which Voltaire would be criticized by some of his fellow *philosophes*; on the other hand, in the 19th century, when Voltaire had come to be widely excoriated in France, by many Catholics at least, as the Antichrist, his *Siècle de Louis XIV* continued to be read as the definitive account of the reign: his pragmatism paid off in the long term. This is of course the behaviour of the perfect courtier, who can insinuate what he thinks without needing to resort to blunt speaking.

An important innovation of the *Siècle de Louis XIV* is the centrality it accords to literature. References to writers are scattered throughout the work, an entire chapter is given over to a history of the great writers of the reign, and Voltaire adds a lengthy catalogue of writers, including many secondary figures, to emphasize the centrality of literature to his narrative. His basic thesis is that this was a golden age for French literature because the king himself encouraged and supported great writers. Leaving aside the questionable truth of this assertion, it is a powerful narrative—and not one designed to endear Voltaire to Louis XV. We should remember that when Louis XIV died in 1715, he had become very unpopular; the most loved monarch at that time was Henry IV, the subject of Voltaire's epic poem. With *Le Siècle de Louis XIV*, Voltaire brings about a revolution in public attitudes and creates the myth of the Sun King that endures to this day. He notes at one point in the work that there were no great historians during Louis XIV's reign—and in saying this, he of course shows his hand. In writing what would remain until Ernest Lavisse's history in the early 20th century the standard account of the reign, Voltaire became himself the great historian of the century of Louis XIV. It was expected that royal historiographers should praise their monarch, but Voltaire makes it abundantly clear that he would much rather have been the Royal Historiographer of Louis XIV than of Louis XV.

A world history

Voltaire's desire to play the role of courtier explains his wish to write the history of monarchs; at the same time, his misgivings and eventual dissatisfaction with court life may help explain why he turned to writing more general history. His other great historical project, begun after *Le Siècle de Louis XIV* in the early 1740s and carried on over many years, was to write a world history, the *Essai sur les mœurs*. Earlier so-called universal histories had usually been confined to the known Christian world and Voltaire, in an overtly polemical gesture, set out to relativize this Christian-centric view. Bossuet's *Discours sur l'histoire universelle* (1681), written to instruct the Dauphin, had famously limited itself to the Christian world and stopped with Charlemagne and so Voltaire began with Charlemagne and sought to embrace all parts of the globe, encapsulating in one narrative sweep the entire history of mankind. He read extremely widely, synthesizing the most reliable accounts as best he could, always with an eye for the revealing detail and an ear for the telling phrase, and the result is one of the great achievements of Enlightenment history writing. The first authorized edition was a best-seller when it appeared in 1756 and the revision and completion of the work occupied Voltaire on and off for the remainder of his life. As the *Essai* moved forward in time, he eventually reached the 17th century, so that after 1768, the *Siècle de Louis XIV* (and its sequel, the *Précis du siècle de Louis XV*) were placed after the *Essai*: his two great historical projects thus merged seamlessly into one. Quickly translated into English and other languages, the *Essai* was widely read across Europe and had a major influence on other great Enlightenment historians like Hume, Robertson, and Gibbon.

A criticism often heard of the *Essai*, made by Voltaire's contemporaries and repeated today, is that its emphasis on the deleterious effects of religion on the course of human affairs is tendentious. Such a critique, while true, completely misses the point. It was precisely Voltaire's intention to write a polemical history and, after centuries of historical writing from a uniquely European and Christian viewpoint, he wants to try the experiment of skewing the perspective (a narrative device he will put to good purpose in his fiction too). His secular, relativizing approach has today so far become the norm that we can all too easily underestimate the scale of his innovation. He is equally innovative in his avowed intention to write the history not just of kings and generals, but of entire cultures. This last aim had long interested him, indeed it was the principle that already underlay his *Letters on the English*, but to apply it more broadly to the whole span of human culture was vastly more ambitious. Even if he is only partially successful in this attempt to write cultural history, he introduces us to a form of historical narrative in which man, and not divine providence, is at the centre.

Educators had long held that their pupils should study the history of the ancient (and not the modern) world, because it was there that one found shining examples of proper moral conduct. Against this view, Voltaire argued strenuously that it was the study of *modern* history that mattered: its lessons were more pertinent to our concerns and the existence of recent printed sources meant that modern history was more reliable. Significantly, modern history began, in Voltaire's view, with the Renaissance and the invention of printing. Earlier history, he felt, was based on little more than story-telling, and in his all-encompassing condemnation of (as he saw them) primitive societies, he lumped together as equivalent the worlds of Homer and the Bible, each as fanciful as the other. Faced by an ancient historical or theological text, Voltaire's greatest term of abuse is to brand it a 'fable' and this explains his fondness for short philosophical tales or 'fables', often constructed as parodies of (bad) histories. The French word *histoire* means both 'history' and 'story', and Voltaire's fictional works are intimately linked to his histories: as a character in his tale *Jeannot et Colin* remarks, 'all ancient history consists of nothing but hackneyed fables'.

The eternal courtier

Voltaire's attempts to assume the role of courtier never ended happily, but the experience was formative in many ways, not least on his work as a historian. Sixteen years older than Louis XV, he did not expect to outlive him, so the king's death in 1774 came as a surprise and the laborious business of paying court to the new king began all over again. His poem *Sésostris* (1776) presents a young Egyptian king who, faced by two goddesses, chooses Wisdom over Pleasure (Voltaire seems to be reworking the plot of *Le Temple de la gloire*): the allegory is cumbersome, but perhaps Voltaire thought that too much subtlety might be wasted on the young Louis XVI. In 1776, the comte de Provence (the king's brother and the future Louis XVIII) decided to stage a celebration in his château de Brunoy for the young queen Marie-Antoinette. But who in the 1770s could still turn out the gallant verses appropriate to a court festivity of the previous century? The answer was obvious and the 82-year-old Voltaire eagerly accepted the commission. *L'Hôte et l'hôtesse* does not pretend to be anything more than an ephemeral work, but it seems to have pleased well enough and that was its purpose. In October 1776, Voltaire wrote to d'Argental that he was happy his verses had been well received by 'the beautiful and brilliant Marie-Antoinette' and that, although he was no courtier, it would do no harm to have her family protect him, a solitary, against 'the wickedness of certain pedants in black robes'. A triumph of hope over experience, perhaps, but Voltaire's desire to have the monarch's approval never left him.

Chapter 6
The Genevan

The mid-1750s mark a new moment of crisis for Voltaire. On the one hand, his reputation had never stood higher: Montesquieu's death in 1755 left him as the undisputed leader of the *philosophes*. Adam Smith, writing that year in the *Edinburgh Review*, speaks of him as a dominant literary figure of the age:

> The most universal genius perhaps which France has ever produced, [he] is acknowledged to be, in almost all species of writing, nearly upon a level with the greatest authors of the last age, who applied themselves chiefly to one.

And yet—the paradox is typical of Voltaire—he had rarely felt more unsettled. After being unceremoniously thrown out of Prussia, following his very public spat with Frederick, he had hoped, rather naively perhaps, that he might return to the French court, so the news in January 1754 that he was not welcome at Versailles struck him, as he wrote in a letter, 'like a bolt of lightening'. His role of courtier in Potsdam had failed miserably and he now needed to find a new role—and a new place to live. Henceforth he would share his life with his niece and companion, Marie-Louise Denis (they had been lovers since the mid-1740s), and she was keen to settle in Lyon, a city with a busy social life, but far enough from the capital for safety. Eventually, however, they settled on Switzerland, then a collection of largely independent republics enjoying a reputation for liberty, and they moved briefly to Lausanne before settling in Geneva. These cities presented obvious attractions: they were French-speaking, their Protestant pastors disliked the Catholic clergy quite as much as Voltaire did, and, a crucial factor in Voltaire's choice, they were both important centres of publishing, with European-wide distribution networks.

Voltaire in Geneva

It was the Genevan printer Gabriel Cramer who found for Voltaire a property on the hillside just outside the city gates of Geneva, a comfortable house with a large garden, commanding fine views down to the Rhône (see Figure 5). Voltaire took out a lease on the house—by a nice irony, he was deemed a Catholic, so could not own property in Geneva—and the erstwhile courtier now became a resident in a Calvinist republic. He moved into his new house in March 1755 and immediately set to work planting fruit trees and ordering asparagus, cultivating the garden in a way that prefigures the ending of *Candide*, the novel which he would write in this house. He named his home 'Les Délices' ('The Delights') and immediately began writing 'Aux Délices' at the head of his letters, relishing the Epicurean ring of the name. The house, now engulfed in the city of Geneva, is today the Musée Voltaire and is well worth visiting though the writer's well-tended garden has been reduced to a small urban park.

Taking occupation of Les Délices, Voltaire began work on a poem, the *Épître de l'auteur, en arrivant dans sa terre près du lac de Genève, en mars 1755*. His hasty and enforced departure from Germany had been a public humiliation, and the poem is a defiant attempt to regain the lost ground, publicly declaring his own liberty at the same time as that of the Swiss republics. Perfect happiness is not to be found among kings, he declares—a daring statement, given what had just happened—and in this poem he

Quererdo sc.
VUE DES DELICES DE M.º DE   VOLTAIRE, PRÈS GENEVE.

Dediée à Monseigneur   *le Duc de Praslin*

Pair de France, Lieutenant *Général des Armées du Roi,*
Chevalier de ses Ordres, Chef *du Conseil Roial des Finances,*
Ministre et   *Secretaire d'Etat, &c &c &c*
          Par son très humble, et très
Se vend chez l'auteur au Nouvel hotel *obeissant Serviteur Signy.*
des Monnoies et chez Didot l'ainée S.t *avec Privilège du Roi*
Germain de l'Auxerrois

5. Voltaire's home 'Les Délices' in Geneva, engraving by F. M. I. Queverdo after a drawing by J. Signy, 1769.

celebrates in parallel the history of Swiss freedom and the Epicurean pleasures to be found in the garden of Les Délices. Edward Gibbon famously describes in his *Memoirs* how as a young man he became acquainted with Voltaire, in late 1756 or early 1757, and after reading a copy of his *Épître de l'auteur*, immediately committed it to memory (see Box 4).

Box 4 How a Voltaire poem became known

I had the satisfaction of seeing the most extraordinary man of the age … : need I add the name of Voltaire? … The Ode which he composed on his first arrival on the banks of the Leman Lake:

O Maison d'Aristippe! O Jardin d'Epicure! etc.

had been imparted as a secret to the Gentleman by whom I was introduced: he allowed me to read it twice; I knew it by heart; as my discretion was not equal to my memory, the author was soon displeased by the circulation of a copy. In writing this trivial anecdote I wished to observe whether my memory was impaired and I have the comfort of finding that every line of the poem is still engraved in fresh and indelible characters.

(Edward Gibbon, *Memoirs of my Life*)

In 1756, Cramer published in Geneva a complete edition of Voltaire's writings, the *Collection complète des œuvres de M. de Voltaire*, in seventeen volumes, a hugely important milestone in Voltaire's literary career. There had been previous collected editions, published in Amsterdam, Dresden, or Paris, but from Voltaire's point of view they had all been unsatisfactory because he had had to supervise them at a distance. Now for the first time, he was able to oversee directly the preparation of his collected writings and to shape the way in which he wanted his *œuvre* to be regarded. The Cramer edition of 1756 is indeed a monument to Voltaire's achievement, but its structure also shows how Voltaire is looking to the future. The first volume is devoted to his epic poem *La Henriade*, as was traditional in these collected sets, and following that one would normally expect to find the classical tragedies. Voltaire breaks with tradition, however, placing at the head of volume two his *Épître de l'auteur, en arrivant dans sa terre*, that is to say, his declaration of Swiss (and his own) liberty; clearly intended as a tribute to his

Swiss hosts, this is also a clear indication that Voltaire is setting out in a new direction.

One of the most interesting innovations of Cramer's *Collection complète* is that two volumes of the seventeen are devoted to miscellaneous short prose pieces, some of them old, but many new and perhaps written to bulk up the edition. Individually, they might seem of little importance, but together, they represent a formidable collection of brief essays: Voltaire will become a prolific writer of these 'short chapters' (as he calls them), brief and pithy philosophical essays which encapsulate an idea, simply and memorably. Voltaire is constantly thinking about literary form, and always the challenge for him is to find a way of matching the medium to his message. His agenda was from the start an unambiguously radical one, arguing in favour of free thought, scepticism, and religious toleration; but aesthetically, he had remained attached to the classical literary genres, the epic poem, the tragedy, and so on, and he spent much energy in the earlier part of his career seeking to 'adapt' these classical literary forms to his own purposes. The canonical literary genres remain vital to him, not least because they are the foundation on which his reputation rests, but now, in his sixties, Voltaire begins to become bolder in his experiments with literary form.

The Lisbon earthquake

Voltaire's successive responses to the catastrophe of the Lisbon earthquake show strikingly how his thinking about literary genre is evolving. In November 1755, a powerful earthquake, followed by a tsunami and devastating fire, destroyed a large part of the city of Lisbon, claiming between 30,000 and 40,000 lives (out of a total population of 200,000). The existence of newspapers, helped by improved road communications, ensured that the earthquake quickly became a European news story and the metaphorical shockwaves were so great that they disrupted even the calm of Voltaire's retreat in Geneva. Horrified by the scale of the destruction,

Voltaire was further appalled by the theologians who immediately began writing tracts declaring that the catastrophe was God's punishment of the sinful people of Lisbon (similar 'arguments' for divine intervention were heard in 2010, following the Haiti earthquake).

Voltaire had long been troubled by the problem of theodicy, the question of why, if God exists and is good, does He allow evil on earth? The Lisbon earthquake of 1755 re-energized his quest for an answer to the problem of evil, and his immediate response was to write a poem of over 200 lines, the *Poème sur le désastre de Lisbonne*. In this emotional response to the disaster, Voltaire defends the idea of Providence and reaffirms his own deist beliefs; he attacks the idea of Optimism, derived from Leibniz, that 'tout est bien' ('all is for the best') and emphasizes the importance of doubt. In revisions to the poem, he added a more hopeful note to the conclusion, but in the end, the poem is interesting as a literary performance making an emotional appeal to its readers rather than for the philosophical solutions that it proposes.

And the literary performance is impressive. Voltaire completed the poem within a matter of weeks, and a manuscript was already circulating in Paris by January 1756. A pirated print edition followed, and only after that did Voltaire instruct Cramer in Geneva to publish the 'official' edition, in which he placed the new poem alongside his earlier (and dryer) philosophical poem on natural religion: *Poèmes sur le désastre de Lisbonne, et sur la Loi naturelle, avec des préfaces, des notes, etc.* Voltaire's skill at producing different versions of a work was a technique for maximizing publicity, and the poem on the Lisbon earthquake enjoyed huge success, more on account of its topicality and the fame of its author than for its intrinsic originality. There were some twenty editions in 1756 alone and the work was translated into many European languages, including Russian and Polish. The

Lisbon earthquake gave Voltaire the opportunity to rehearse his views before a European-wide audience and he seized it with both hands.

Voltaire's fiction

Voltaire's second response to the Lisbon earthquake took longer to incubate and appeared in the form of a novel: *Candide* was published by Cramer in Geneva in early 1759. Today, it is the most read of all his works, a fact which would have astonished his contemporaries and no doubt Voltaire himself. In fact he had been interested in story-telling, though not in publishing his stories, from an early stage. He had first composed tales for the duchesse du Maine in the years 1714–15, and there was a second phase of fictional creativity in the late 1730s, but all of these stories were intended strictly as social entertainments. Only in the late 1740s, following his period of favour at the French court, when his reputation as a poet, tragedian, and historian was secure, did Voltaire decide to publish a work of fiction.

His oriental novel *Zadig* first came out in 1747 and in the following five years, up to 1752, a further four fictions were published: two stories which have their origins in the Cirey period, *Le Monde comme il va* and the 'scientific' tale *Micromégas*, and two other shorter pieces, *Memnon* and the *Lettre d'un Turc*. In addition, from 1751, Voltaire began to publish philosophical dialogues, and the appearance of these more playful works marks an important step in the way in which he wished to be seen as an author. Firmly established as a writer, elected to the Academy, received at court, he finally seemed able to relax and show a less formal and arguably more innovative side to his creativity. The experience of court, first at Versailles and then at Potsdam, may have played a role: after the relatively secluded period at Cirey, life at court involved conveying ideas in an entertaining and informal manner, and Voltaire's gift for communication with a large public may have its roots in his ability to thrive in the elite community of the court.

Three of these early fictions, *Le Monde comme il va*, *Memnon*, and *Zadig*, all deal centrally with the problem of evil and all employ the fictional device of an angel who descends, *ex machina*, to expound the Optimist cause to a bemused hero. So *Candide* (1759) is his fourth fictional attempt to address the question of evil in the world, but now, after the Lisbon earthquake, he writes a full-length novel, in which the spokesman for Optimism is no longer an angel but a human being. The philosophical position confusingly known as Optimism derives from the German philosopher Leibniz. What seems evil to human beings appears so only because of their limited perspective; from God's point of view, the argument runs, the world we inhabit is 'the best of all possible worlds'; to put it another way, evil does not really exist when viewed in a broader context. This view, albeit in a simplified form, was popularized by the English poet Alexander Pope, whose *Essay on Man* (1734) was widely read across Europe.

Candide, like so many novels of the period, presents us with a hero travelling in search of truth. The typical 18th-century hero is a child of Locke; he is meant to learn empirically from experience as his journey through life progresses. Candide starts out suitably as a blank sheet (his name means 'white' in Latin), but it is by no means clear that he learns from experience. He has been taught by his German professor Pangloss, in a phrase that has become proverbial, that 'all is for the best in the best of all possible worlds'. And he is subject to a crash course in evil and human cruelty: he staggers from battlefield to earthquake, witnessing evil in every form, and always mouthing the party line that this is all for the best. In this surreal journey, the joke is that Candide does not really learn and so the novel is typically read as a satire on Leibnizian Optimism.

It is that, up to a point, but it is also more. Near the end of the novel, Candide asks Pangloss if, after all that has happened, he still believes in his Optimist mantra:

> —Well, my dear Pangloss, Candide said to him, when you were hanged, dissected, beaten and forced to row in the galleys, did you still believe that everything was for the best in this world?

> —I hold to my first opinion, replied Pangloss; for after all I am a philosopher: it would not be right for me to change my mind since Leibniz cannot possibly be wrong, and in any case pre-established harmony, along with the plenum and subtle matter, is the finest thing in the world.

Candide may not learn from experience, but he does shed tears when confronted by the misery of the amputated slave who works on a sugar plantation. Pangloss, on the other hand, remains inhuman in his rigid attachment to dogma, and the reader can only conclude that all metaphysical systems are laughable and that everything should be doubted. The true object of mockery here is not simply Optimism, or any other belief system for that matter: Voltaire's real mockery is reserved for those human beings who deny their essential humanity by clinging to beliefs which are demonstrably harmful and rationally unprovable.

This is hardly a new idea, though undoubtedly it is an important one, and *Candide* hammers it home with unequalled vigour and wit. What is truly subversive in this novel is the unbridled sense of the comic. If the authorities condemned the novel, it was not because of some abstract discussion of Leibniz, but because it made fun of them and of all authorities. Candide comes close to being eaten by savages when he is mistaken for a Jesuit, and the cannibals' cry 'Mangeons du jésuite!' ('Let's eat some Jesuit') so delighted contemporary readers that the French expression immediately acquired proverbial status. The novel took Europe by storm and no fewer than seventeen editions appeared in the first year of publication; three different English translations appeared in London in the course of 1759. If *Candide* is now Voltaire's most widely translated work, it is because the zany and surreal qualities of its bitter-sweet comedy seem to speak to all cultures and to all periods.

For the same reasons, *Candide* has attracted eminent artists and illustrators, who continue to reinterpret the work. Paul Klee, Alfred Kubin, and Rockwell Kent have all produced radically different readings, and the tradition continues: Chris Ware, the American cartoonist, has reinvented *Candide* as a graphic novel (2005), while Quentin Blake (2011) emphasizes its traditional comic virtues. In the 18th century there were several continuations of the novel and modern writers remain fascinated by the text. George Bernard Shaw wrote his own take on *Candide*, entitled *The Adventures of the Black Girl in her Search for God* (1932), in which Shaw himself ends up as an Irish labourer cultivating the garden alongside Voltaire (see Box 5), while the Sicilian novelist Leonardo Sciascia, in *Candido* (1977), imagines his hero making his way in post-war Italy, torn between the rival ideologies of Communism and Christianity. Many other novels—Cormac McCarthy's *The Road* (2006), Salman Rushdie's *Two Years Eight Months & Twenty-Eight Nights* (2015)—seem to gesture to *Candide*, even if they are not precise imitations. No surprise, then, that two students from Chicago have 'retold' *Candide* in a series of tweets (2009). There have been numerous stage versions, beginning with a Paisiello opera in 1784, but it is Leonard Bernstein's 'musical operetta' *Candide* (1956) which has enjoyed the most enduring success: originally interpreted in the USA as a satire on the McCarthy trials of the 1950s, the musical became, in Robert Carsen's Paris production in 2006, a satire on the leaders of the Iraq War. The possibilities of human folly seem infinite and we go on reading *Candide*.

Box 5 Shaw's Black Girl discusses God with Voltaire

She came to a prim little villa with a very amateurish garden which was being cultivated by a wizened old gentleman...

'Excuse me, baas' she said: 'May I speak to you?'

'What do you want' said the old gentleman.

'I want to ask my way to God' she said; 'and as you have the most knowing face I have ever seen, I thought I would ask you.'

'Come in' said he. 'I have found, after a good deal of consideration, that the best place to seek God is in a garden. You can dig for Him here.'

'That is not my idea of seeking for God at all' said the black girl, disappointed. 'I will go on, thank you.'

'Has your own idea, as you call it, led you to Him yet?'

'No' said the black girl, stopping: 'I cannot say that it has. But I do not like your idea.'

'Many people who have found God have not liked Him and have spent the rest of their lives running away from Him. Why do you suppose that you would like Him?'

'I don't know' said the black girl. 'But the missionary has a line of poetry that says that we needs must love the highest when we see it.'

'That poet was a fool' said the old gentleman. 'We hate it; we crucify it; we poison it with hemlock; we chain it to a stake and burn it alive. All my life I have striven in my little way to do God's work and teach His enemies to laugh at themselves; but if you told me God was coming down the road I should creep into the nearest mousehole and not dare to breathe until He had passed.'

(George Bernard Shaw, *The Adventures of the Black Girl in her Search for God*, 1933)

Voltaire takes leave of Geneva

Voltaire's literary response to the Lisbon earthquake took two very different forms, both of them highly popular with a European-wide readership—we have here a writer in full command of his public. But it is interesting to compare these two literary productions. Voltaire's immediate response was cast in the traditional form of a philosophical poem; and, despite its undoubted success, this was to be his last major philosophical work in verse. His second response, which grew more slowly in his mind, was a work of prose fiction, a satirical novel of extraordinary originality. The *Poème sur le désastre de Lisbonne*, at least in retrospect, looks like a dead end; it is *Candide* which points forward to the continuing literary experiments of the next decade.

The critique of Adam Smith quoted at the start of this chapter is telling, for to suggest that Voltaire is 'acknowledged to be, in almost all species of writing, nearly upon a level with the greatest authors of the last age' comes close to damning with faint praise. According to this view, while unequalled in his command of a wide range of established literary genres, Voltaire seemingly does not dominate in any and has not developed his own fully distinctive literary style. This was perhaps a fair criticism of him in 1755, but it is hard to think that Adam Smith would have written in quite the same terms five years later, after that period of intense creativity for Voltaire which included the composition of *Candide*.

The Swiss idyll, so confidently articulated in the *Épître de l'auteur, en arrivant dans sa terre*, soon palled. Voltaire's theatrical performances caused tensions with the Genevan authorities who disapproved of theatre in general, and Protestant clerics turned out for the most part to be as fanatical as their Catholic counterparts. The monarchist Voltaire was never going to be comfortable in the longer term living as a resident in a theological republic and in 1758 he purchased a large estate at Ferney, very close to Geneva, but just across the border on French soil. Voltaire, at last, would own the house he lived in and no one would be able to call him an exile.

Chapter 7
The campaigner

In December 1759, the *philosophe* Grimm wrote that Voltaire was 'le premier homme de l'Europe' ('the first man of Europe'), and in the same vein, Oliver Goldsmith described him the following year as 'the poet and philosopher of Europe': Voltaire's fame as a writer could, it seemed, grow no greater. He was, as Jean-Jacques Rousseau meanly remarked in his *Confessions*, 'weighed down by fame and prosperity'. Voltaire had already lived more than the average span for a man of the 18th century, and if he had died in 1760, we would remember him today as one of the greatest French authors of the century, a historian and playwright, and the author of *Candide*. No one then could have predicted that in the course of the 1760s Voltaire's standing as an author would change radically and that he would reinvent himself as a political activist and public celebrity of a wholly new type.

In the years after 1760, Voltaire finally became a Voltairean, triumphantly finding the voice as a public intellectual that has ever since characterized him. In Protestant Geneva he had been a tenant, unable to own property, but now he acquired a handsome château at Ferney in France, adjacent to the border with Geneva (the village, now a small town, has restyled itself Ferney-Voltaire). The owner of his property and lord of the manor enjoying feudal rights over the local community, Voltaire was, at last, living on French soil and on his own terms, far from Paris and conveniently close to the printing presses of Geneva. He had become very wealthy (through investments and making loans) and his wealth provided not just a luxurious lifestyle, but also, more importantly, a guarantee of independence. As he would later write, 'I have made myself a king at home.' Voltaire was now universally recognized as the Patriarch of Ferney.

Malagrida: a public victim

In October 1761, Voltaire read in the *Gazette de France* about an auto-da-fé that had occurred in Lisbon the previous month, in which the Inquisition had executed some forty-odd people, including an elderly Jesuit, Father Malagrida. Voltaire had no reason to defend a Jesuit—least of all a Jesuit who had become famous for arguing that the Lisbon earthquake of 1755 was God's judgement on man—but the spectacle of the Inquisition putting to death one of their own piqued his sense of irony. Voltaire tried hard to find out more details of the case, which was a complicated one: unable to find Malagrida guilty of attempted regicide, the court had eventually condemned the Jesuit instead for heresy, on the basis of extremely flimsy, even ludicrous, evidence. There were political machinations which Voltaire could not have fully known but which he suspected: in reality Malagrida was guilty of being an opponent of the prime minister, the future marquis de Pombal, who feared the growing influence of the Jesuits at the court of Joseph I. Whatever the precise facts, the burning of Malagrida was clearly an excessive punishment and the justification given for it utterly absurd—an uncomfortable echo of the Lisbon auto-da-fé in *Candide*. As Voltaire wrote to his Paris friends, the comte and comtesse d'Argental: 'I don't mind so much that they burned brother Malagrida, but I do feel sorry for the half-dozen Jews who were grilled. An auto-da-fé still in this century! Whatever will Candide say?' Here was a clear case of life imitating art.

In late 1761, Voltaire published a brief satire about the Malagrida affair entitled the *Sermon du rabbin Akib*, in which he adopted the voice of a Jew, and the form of the sermon, to lament the cruelty inflicted by Catholics on one another. As Voltaire's 'Jewish' speaker makes clear, intolerance seems to be a Christian invention. This magnificently ironical work was an instant success: the short brochure was quick to reprint and easy to translate, and its brevity made it possible to reproduce it as a newspaper article. Such was the print industry in the 18th century that a work like this could very quickly acquire a life of its own, and the *Sermon* circulated widely not only in France but also in England, where it was much reprinted in the provincial press. Pombal, concerned with public opinion and anxious to project abroad a positive 'Enlightened' image of Portugal, published in French translation both the sentence against Malagrida and a justification for it. But too late: thanks to Voltaire's satire, Malagrida had already achieved fame across Europe as a victim of the Inquisition. From Pombal's point of view, the publicity war was lost in advance; Voltaire was victorious.

The Malagrida case marks in retrospect an important turning point. An incident in far-off Lisbon became known to Voltaire at Ferney: it grew into a 'news story' thanks to the efficiency of the 18th-century press and the appetite of the growing reading public. Voltaire quickly grasped the polemical (and blackly comic) potential of the story of one group of Catholics using, for their own political reasons, trumped-up charges and a faulty judicial process to execute a fellow group of Catholics. Not only is religious faith called into question by these events, so are the due processes of the legal system and civil society: the laws should protect a man, even a Jesuit, from injustice, not aid and abet the intolerant and the bigoted. And meanwhile Voltaire learned an important lesson about the power of the press to sway public opinion.

The Calas affair

The case of Malagrida paved the way for the Calas affair that was soon to make headlines across Europe. The cruel execution of

Malagrida had taken place in a foreign country and it did, in Voltaire's portrayal at least, have a bleakly comic quality. The Calas affair was closer to home and not in the least comic. Jean Calas was a Protestant merchant in his early sixties who lived with his family in Toulouse. In October 1761, his eldest son Marc-Antoine was discovered dead at home—in all probability a suicide, which shamed members of the family sought to cover up. The judicial authorities decided, on the basis of hearsay evidence, that the young man had been murdered by his father because he was proposing to convert to Catholicism. The *parlement* of Toulouse, by eight votes to five, decided on torture and the death penalty, and in March 1762 Jean Calas was executed, declaring his innocence to the very end. The execution was gruesome: Calas was first tortured by being stretched and drawn by weights, then forced to swallow large quantities of water; he steadfastly refused to name his accomplices, declaring that 'where there is no crime, there cannot be accomplices'; next the executioner smashed his limbs, one by one, then a winch was used to dislocate the vertebrae of his neck; only when the body was literally broken was it fastened to a wheel and put atop a pole for the edification of the public in the Place Saint-Georges in Toulouse. By a secret dispensation, the court allowed Calas to be strangled to death after only two hours of torment.

Voltaire first heard about the case at the end of March and he made contact with two of Calas's children to find out more; the family was in a desperate plight since the judgement prevented them from inheriting their father's property and possessions. His sense of outrage grew as it became increasingly clear to him that proper judicial process had been ignored and that the decisions of the Catholic judges had been motivated by religious prejudice. He prepared a series of documents, mainly in the form of letters, aimed at demonstrating Jean Calas's innocence and these *Pièces originales* were published in early July. Voltaire kept up the pressure, notably with a campaign of letter writing to people of influence in the capital, until in March 1763, in what would prove a decisive turning point, the privy council at Versailles allowed an appeal against the decision of the *parlement* in Toulouse.

Meanwhile Voltaire was working on a longer and more ambitious work, to be published later in 1763, the *Traité sur la tolérance*. The opening chapter recounts the circumstances of Calas's condemnation, putting much emphasis on the 'fanaticism' of the devout Catholics in the provincial city of Toulouse, and the book then develops over twenty-five chapters into a broader manifesto for religious toleration. Voltaire uses a wide range of historical examples drawn from Greek and Roman antiquity and from China, and discusses toleration in the Jewish tradition as well as in the teachings of Jesus, to conclude that toleration is a universal principle. On several occasions, Voltaire refers to *le droit humain* ('human right')—the first time that this expression occurs in his works—which is not quite the same as the 'human rights' that will be invoked in the French Revolution three decades later, but is clearly nudging in that direction. Nature teaches us that we should treat others as we would wish to be treated by them, argues Voltaire; according to this 'universal principle', intolerance cannot be part of *le droit humain*. In this passage, Voltaire alludes to the Inquisition and the example of Portugal shows that he still has Malagrida at the back of his mind, not to mention the lampooning of the Lisbon Inquisition in *Candide*:

> Now it is hard to see how, following this principle, one man could say to another: 'Believe what I believe, and what you do not believe, otherwise you will perish'. This is what they say in Portugal, in Spain, in Goa.

Voltaire was hardly the first to write in favour of toleration and he would certainly have known John Locke's *Letter Concerning Toleration* (1689). But whereas Locke writes from the standpoint of a philosopher and political theorist, Voltaire adopts a more journalistic stance, beginning empirically with contemporary events and drawing commonsense conclusions reinforced by historical examples. The *Traité* has extraordinary immediacy and its publication caused a frenzy. Voltaire kept it under wraps for as long as he could, sending copies only to intimate friends—in December 1763, even his close ally D'Alembert complained that he had not been able to find a copy. But of course in showing such extreme caution, Voltaire was also inflating the demand for his work. In March 1764, David Hume, then in Paris, noted that copies of the *Traité* were hard to find—obviously he was keen to read it too; pirated copies soon began to appear in other French towns and the book was all but unstoppable. More than that, it was successful, for Voltaire's activism had a direct influence on the course of political events. In June 1764, the privy council overruled completely the judgements of the Toulouse courts; and finally in 1765, three years after Calas's execution, all members of the family were pronounced innocent of all charges.

This was an enormous triumph for the party of the *philosophes*, a victory for reason over the forces of obscurantism, and Voltaire was hailed as the man who by the force of his pen had 'saved' the Calas family. His crusade for religious tolerance was all the more effective because he had identified a single enemy and a single objective. The enemy was *l'Infâme* ('the despicable'), a term that Voltaire first coined in exchanges with Frederick to describe the unacceptable manifestations of religion (superstition, dogmatism, fanaticism); the objective was simply to attack *l'Infâme* relentlessly, on every possible occasion. And as with all good campaigns, Voltaire created a slogan: *Écrasez l'Infâme!* ('Crush the despicable!'). Voltaire creates this exhortation at the time of the Calas affair and uses it repeatedly in letters to close friends, employing the expression to sign off literally hundreds of letters and shortening it often to *Ecrlinf*. The censors who were kept busy reading the mail passing between Geneva and Paris were confused and they allegedly reported to their superiors the existence of a suspicious individual living in Switzerland called Ecrelinf: as often in his tussles with authority, Voltaire got the last laugh.

The *Dictionnaire philosophique portatif*

After the *Traité sur la tolérance*, which detailed the history of intolerance, Voltaire broadened his attack on *l'Infâme* in an even more ambitious work, the *Dictionnaire philosophique portatif*. The first edition, containing seventy-three articles, created huge scandal on its first appearance in 1764 and there then ensued a most extraordinary campaign of letter writing in which Voltaire announced to all the world that, of course, he knew nothing at all about this new book. The sceptical critique of the Bible is dominant in the *Dictionnaire* and Voltaire is strongly influenced by the model of the Huguenot Pierre Bayle's *Dictionnaire historique et critique*, first published in 1697, and much read during the Enlightenment.

Opening with the article 'Abraham', the patriarch of Ferney goes head to head with Abraham, the first patriarch of Israel, starting as he means to go on with a full-out attack on the whole biblical tradition. In the Koran, Islam is referred to as 'the religion of Abraham', so to begin with the person seen as a founding figure of not just one but two faiths is a bold opening: from the outset, Christianity's claim to uniqueness is relativized. Voltaire's particular focus is on the Old Testament and he shows that the world-view which it presents, far from being inspired by God, derives from earlier pagan structures of myth; it paints a picture of God which is absurd and cruel, and expounds views that are repugnant, even immoral. This Old Testament world-view is shown to be at odds with the findings of modern science and to be incoherent and contradictory, a work of fiction in fact. This critique of the Judaeo-Christian tradition is widely shared by the free-thinkers of the Enlightenment, but none of the other *philosophes* could rival Voltaire's biblical erudition, which has its roots in his discussions of the Bible with Émilie Du Châtelet at Cirey. He knows the enemy better than anyone else and writes with a depth of historical knowledge (even if he presents it tendentiously) which cannot fail to impress, even at times intimidate, the reader.

Voltaire is gentler with the New Testament: he may not believe in its metaphysical underpinning, but he is broadly in sympathy with its ethical principles. Throughout, Voltaire 'desacralizes' religious faith, subjecting it to the pragmatic test of how it helps mankind. So in the article 'Baptism', he considers the sacrament as an image: 'In itself, any sign is immaterial: God attaches his grace to the sign he is pleased to choose'—in other words, claims to transcendence are circular and meaningless. What matters is practical, ethical action: 'Philosophy'—by which he means reasoned reflection—'brings peace to the soul' (article 'Fanaticism'). Alongside the articles on religion, a smaller important sub-set deals with philosophy, politics, and justice—this last theme acquires increasing prominence in subsequent revisions. Voltaire offers us in sum a critique of the Judaeo-Christian tradition and an alternative system of belief grounded in reason. All mankind can acknowledge a Supreme Being, who created the universe and who punishes evil. What more do we need? What matters for Voltaire is the practical effect of this belief: the happiness of individuals, prospering in a tolerant civil society. Article after article makes reference to the Supreme Being and yet there is no article 'Deism'—for the simple reason that deism is at the core of the whole edifice of the *Dictionnaire*.

It would be wrong to give an impression of the *Dictionnaire* as a work that is fixed or stable. Voltaire's aim is to provoke us into thought and argument, to liberate us from impostors of every sort who would deny us the freedom to use our own reason. In subsequent editions he continued to add articles to the *Dictionnaire*, so that by 1769 it filled two volumes and contained 118 articles: no longer 'portable' (*portatif*), the word was dropped from the title. The *Dictionnaire* prompted many critics to write rebuttals and the additions that Voltaire made to his work (new articles, or additions to existing articles) are often ripostes to these criticisms. The dialogue inaugurated by the book thus continues as a dialogue with its critics and Voltaire usually contrives to have the last word.

After 1769 Voltaire leaves the *Dictionnaire philosophique* on one side, to concentrate on a new project, the *Questions sur l'Encyclopédie*. This is another alphabetical dictionary and it appeared in seven volumes, between 1770 and 1772. A best-seller at the time, though little studied since, this work is Voltaire's last great prose masterpiece. In part a continuation of the *Dictionnaire*, in part a dialogue with some articles of the *Encyclopédie*, the *Questions* move beyond the anti-biblical critique central to the earlier *Dictionnaire* to embrace all the subjects that interested Voltaire; some of the articles recycle texts he had written decades earlier, while others tackle new topics like economics or law and justice. The work as a whole, held together ostensibly by its alphabetical structure and in fact by the force of the author's personality and his familiar narrative voice and style, amounts to a polemical tour de force that is also a summation of Voltaire's achievement.

Like others of Voltaire's longer prose works, the *Letters on the English*, for example, or his universal history, the *Essai sur les mœurs*, the *Dictionnaire*, and the *Questions sur l'Encyclopédie* are not 'finished' works, but works in progress. The conclusion to the article 'Sensation' in the *Dictionnaire* is characteristic: 'What can we conclude from all that? You who can read and think, you conclude.' Voltaire always privileges movement over stasis, perhaps on the principle that it is harder to hit a moving target, perhaps because he is interested more in provoking questions than in shaping answers, perhaps because he dislikes putting a final full stop at the end of any discussion. For both moral and political reasons, he favours forms that hold off definitive pronouncements and thereby encourage scepticism and tolerance. Whatever the reasons, there is a fundamental fluidity and openness about the way he structures his longer prose works that makes them seem surprisingly modern.

The invention of the 'affair'

The Calas affair was a defining event in Voltaire's career: it produced a radically new public image of the writer and gave him a new awareness of the power of public opinion. Such was Voltaire's reputation that other 'affairs' were to follow, with depressing regularity. Pierre Paul Sirven, like Calas a Protestant from the Languedoc, was accused in 1762 of murdering his mentally unstable daughter, and again the Toulouse *parlement* was involved: Voltaire's untiring campaigning led to Sirven and his entire family being fully cleared—but only in 1771. Then there was the comte de Lally, the Irish Jacobite turned French military man, who surrendered at Pondicherry in 1761 and was beheaded in 1766 for treason. Lally's son pleaded with Voltaire to help him clear his father's name. Again, the process was protracted, and finally the news that Lally's father had been posthumously exonerated reached Voltaire as he lay on his deathbed in Paris in 1778: he remained a campaigner to his dying breath.

The most disturbing case—disturbing because Voltaire felt himself personally implicated—was that of the chevalier de La Barre. In 1766, in Abbeville in Picardy, this young man, together with two friends, was accused of causing damage to a crucifix, of singing anti-religious songs, and of showing disrespect to a religious procession. La Barre's room was searched and a number of compromising books were found, including, so it was alleged, the *Dictionnaire philosophique*. At the ensuing trial, it was suggested that this book had exercised a corrupting influence on the young man; he was found guilty and condemned to have his tongue torn out, to be beheaded (a concession to a gentleman), and to have his body burned on a pyre along with a copy of the offending book. This sentence was confirmed by a court in Paris and La Barre was duly executed on 1 July 1766, his body burned along with a copy of the *Dictionnaire philosophique*. The legal process and punishment exemplified all too clearly the vices and prejudices laid bare in that volume, not least the cruelty of religious fanatics and the lack of simple Christian charity in some believers. The fact that the authorities felt the need to burn publicly the *Dictionnaire philosophique* rather made Voltaire's point: they were burning him in proxy. A few days later, on 7 July, just after hearing the news of La Barre's execution, Voltaire wrote to Damilaville:

> My dear brother, my heart is withered, I am crushed. I never imagined that anyone would blame this most silly and unrestrained piece of madness on people who preach only wisdom and purity of morals. I am tempted to go and die in some foreign land where men are less unjust. I am silent, I have too much to say.

Voltaire did not remain silent for long. He circulated an anonymous letter, allegedly sent from Abbeville and dated 7 July, and then he wrote the *Relation de la mort du chevalier de La Barre*, dated 15 July, a longer piece, ostensibly addressed to the Italian jurist Beccaria, who in 1764 had just published his *Dei delitti e delle pene* (*On Crimes and Punishments*), a landmark in Enlightenment thinking on judicial reform. Eventually, Duval, the investigating magistrate, was dismissed and the other two defendants were acquitted: too late for the chevalier de La Barre, but Voltaire enjoyed a victory of sorts.

Voltaire's brilliance at conducting these campaigns to rouse public opinion should not blind us to his limitations. From a modern perspective, when we read the details of the punishments doled out to Calas or La Barre, we can only be horrified by the barbaric savagery condoned by the judicial processes of the *ancien régime*. Voltaire's attack on these miscarriages of justice is not—at least not to begin with—motivated by the cruelty of the punishments involved. He has an intellectual distaste for the way in which (false) religion warps men's intellect and is horrified by judges who make irrational judgements based on religious prejudice. In an article 'Certain, certitude' (1770) in the *Questions sur l'Encyclopédie*, he discusses miscarriages of justice, such as when Monbailli and his wife were wrongfully and cruelly executed for the murder of his mother, as examples of how judicial certitude may lead to errors of judgement. The aristocratic jurist Montesquieu had already attacked the practice of torture, in admittedly sober terms, in his *De l'esprit des lois* (1748), yet that discussion seems not to impinge on Voltaire's early reactions to the Calas trial. Lynn Hunt has argued that the concern with human rights that emerges in this period is closely linked to the striking focus on sensibility in contemporary literature, but this emotional response to the cruelty of torture may not have been Voltaire's primary motivation when he began these campaigns.

Voltaire did however have a very sharp eye for the ways that contemporary thinking was evolving: Beccaria's work, when it appeared in Morellet's French translation in 1766, caused a sensation, not least because it appeared in the wake of the debate about the Calas affair. In a naked attempt to regain the initiative, fearing he might be overshadowed, Voltaire speedily wrote a *Commentary* on Beccaria's work—in fact not a 'commentary' at all, but a substantial essay on the cruelty of the judicial system in *ancien régime* France. The work appeared in the autumn of 1766 and was subsequently often printed together with Beccaria's treatise. Voltaire had identified a shift in public opinion and, thanks to some fast footwork, managed to place himself on the right side of history. By the end of the century, the abolition of torture had become a major topic of discussion all across Europe and Voltaire's influence on that debate, as an activist rather than as a profound thinker, was considerable.

In all these battles, Voltaire's distinctive weapon is ridicule. His voice is instantly recognizable and he handles irony and sarcasm more brilliantly than anyone else. He mocks his adversaries, attributing to them absurd and illogical reasoning, as in the *Traité sur la tolérance*, when he 'explains' how the Catholic Church defended the St Bartholomew's Day massacre of 1572, when Catholics in Paris assassinated thousands of Huguenots in an orchestrated wave of mob violence:

> The successor of St Peter and his council of cardinals cannot be wrong; they endorsed, celebrated, sanctioned the actions of St Bartholomew's Day; therefore this action was most holy; therefore, of two equally pious assassins, the one who disembowelled eighty pregnant Huguenot women has earned twice as much eternal glory as the one who only disembowelled twelve…

Persons in authority fear, more than anything else, public ridicule and Voltaire's stylistic bravura turned the magistrates of Toulouse into figures of fun. If the Paris courts overruled the provincial judges, it was in part because they had to put a stop to the corrosive ridicule that he had unleashed. Montesquieu may have attacked torture already in the 1740s, but no one particularly remembered the attack; after Voltaire had attacked the Toulouse magistrates, no one could ever forget it.

In the early 1760s, Voltaire in effect invents the 'affair'. His actions were profoundly subversive to the *ancien régime* legal system, for justice was carried out in the name of the king and in strict secrecy: for example, an accused did not have the right to hear the evidence against him before his trial. From a sociological standpoint, as Élisabeth Claverie has shown, justice was delivered very much according to the religious and social status of the accused. Voltaire's campaigns on behalf of Calas and La Barre turned these rules inside out: the public nature of the campaign meant that the 'privacy' of royal justice had been breached; and his invocation of general interest transcended the interests of any particular social category. In the *Traité sur la tolérance*, Voltaire repeatedly invokes *le genre humain* ('mankind') to give general, universal, import to the specific facts of a particular case. In this way the public arena becomes transformative in turning a trial into an affair.

Public opinion

The invention of the 'affair' is arguably Voltaire's greatest achievement of the Ferney years, and his remarkable victory in the Calas affair gives him a wholly new understanding of the power of public opinion. In 1763, in his *Remarques pour servir de supplément à l'Essai sur les mœurs*, he speaks of the 'power of opinion', and the idea resurfaces in his tragedy *Olympie* (1764): 'Opinion is all-powerful; it has condemned you.' The challenge now is for the *philosophes* to channel the forces of opinion, as Voltaire clearly recognizes (in a letter of 1764): 'Opinion rules the world, but in the long run it is the philosophers who shape opinion.' In 1765 Grimm and Diderot promoted the plan to sell by subscription an engraving of *La Malheureuse Famille Calas* (see Figure 6), based on a drawing by the artist Carmontelle, as a

LA MALHEUREUSE FAMILLE CALAS.
La Mère, les Deux Filles, avec Jeanne Viguiere, leur bonne Servante, le Fils et son ami, le jeune Lavaysse.

6. *La Malheureuse Famille Calas*, engraving by J.-B. Delafosse after a drawing by L. C. Carmontelle, 1765.

means of providing financial support for the Calas family who had been left destitute. Here is a project that helped the cause of the *philosophes* as much as it helped members of the Calas family, and Voltaire subscribed for twelve copies. A late comic engraving by Vivant Denon depicting Voltaire in his bed surrounded by friends shows us that the print *La Malheureuse Famille Calas* hung over his bed where he could see it every morning when he woke up (see Figure 7).

In this campaign to shape public opinion, Voltaire needed to communicate with the widest possible number and to remain constantly in the public eye. He does this first and foremost, as we have seen, by means of his publications: he writes with fluency and speed, and the works flood from his pen—Grimm refers, not entirely flatteringly, to the 'Ferney factory'. Voltaire specialized in short, jagged literary forms (the pamphlet, the story, the article),

7. *Le Déjeuner de Ferney*, engraving by Lafitte after a drawing from nature by Vivant Denon, 4 July 1775.

perfectly adapted to polemical purposes, which he then sometimes reworked and republished in newly created anthologies—he had all the time to remain before his public. Letter writing was another essential tool and he wrote many letters every day to friends and people in high places; we know of over 16,000 letters by Voltaire, making this correspondence one of the most significant in European literature. Relatively few of these letters could be categorized as strictly private and personal—not even those in which he discusses his state of health, a lifelong obsession with Voltaire; very often they address a wider audience than the mere addressee, and he wrote in the full knowledge that a letter from him would be read aloud, shown to friends, and perhaps passed around and copied.

The role of visitors was important too: the château de Ferney had become a standard feature of many grand tours and visitors passing through Geneva felt obliged to call on the most famous writer of the age. Voltaire lived in high style and was famously hospitable—he described himself in these years as 'the innkeeper of Europe'—and visitors, like the young and impressionable James Boswell, were very likely to put on record afterwards their impressions of the great man (see Box 6). Voltaire was the source of endless stories and anecdotes, as when in 1761 he rebuilt the village church just in front of his château and put up an engraved inscription *Deo erexit Voltaire*, 'Voltaire built this for God' (see Figure 8). The *London Magazine* in 1773 reported that Voltaire 'says this is the only church in Christendom dedicated to God' and they might have added that Voltaire's name was engraved in larger letters than God's. The point about this kind of anecdote was that it was designed to be talked about and reported in the press. When in 1768 and 1769 Voltaire took Easter communion in the local church, this ostensibly private act suddenly became a topic of national debate: was the old man feeble of mind? Or was this provocative impiety? Voltaire enjoyed keeping everyone guessing: he had a showman's shrewd sense of communication.

Box 6 James Boswell recalls his visit to Ferney in December 1764

I returned yesterday to this enchanted castle. The magician appeared a very little before dinner. But in the evening he came into the drawing room in great spirits. I placed myself by him…He was all brilliance. He gave me continued flashes of wit. I got him to speak English…and when he talked our language he was animated with the soul of a Briton. He had bold flights. He had humour…He swore bloodily, as was the fashion when he was in England. He hummed a ballad; he repeated nonsense. Then he talked of our Constitution with a noble enthusiasm. I was proud to hear this from the mouth of an illustrious Frenchman. At last we came upon religion. Then did he rage. The company went to supper. Monsieur de Voltaire and I remained in the drawing room with a great Bible before us; and if ever two mortal men disputed with vehemence, we did…The daring bursts of his ridicule confounded my understanding. He stood like an orator of ancient Rome…He went too far. His aged frame trembled beneath him. He cried, 'Oh, I am very sick; my head turns round,' and he let himself gently fall upon an easy chair. He recovered. I resumed our conversation but changed the tone…I demanded of him an honest confession of his real sentiments. He gave it me with candour and with a mild eloquence which touched my heart…He expressed his veneration—his love—of the Supreme Being, and his entire resignation to the will of Him who is All-Wise. He expressed his desire to resemble the Author of Goodness by being good himself. His sentiments go no farther. He does not inflame his mind with grand hopes of the immortality of the soul. He says it may be, but knows nothing of it. And his mind is in perfect tranquillity. I was moved; I was sorry. I doubted his sincerity. I called to him with emotion, 'Are you sincere? Are you really sincere?' He answered, 'Before God, I am.' Then with the fire of him whose tragedies have so often shone on the theatre of Paris, he said: 'I suffer much. But I suffer with patience and resignation; not as a Christian—but as a man.'

Voltaire

8. Voltaire's inscription on the chapel at Ferney: 'Voltaire erected this to God'.

By this stage in his career, Voltaire's prose style had made him inimitable, while his celebrity had made him untouchable. His mastery of the 'media' of the day—essentially the press, but also the circulation of manuscripts, including letters—further enhanced his reputation. This final role of patriarch is his most successful performance—one might say it is his ultimate self-creation—and it shapes definitively the image of Voltaire that has come down to posterity. We forget the hesitations and failures of his earlier life and we remember the patriarch of Ferney.

Voltaire was relentless in attacking the absurdities of religious intolerance: his strength lies perhaps in the simplicity (and timelessness) of the message. Time and time again, he repeated the same examples, hammering away with withering irony at the same targets. If a fanatic is, as Churchill said, 'one who can't change his mind and won't change the subject', then we would have to say that Voltaire is a fanatic in combating fanaticism. He would be remembered for ever after as *l'homme aux Calas* ('the man of the Calas family'), and in the final months of his life when he returned to Paris, there were cries of *l'homme aux Calas* as he walked through the streets. Even Diderot, who did not always find Voltaire easy to like, was full of praise for *l'homme aux Calas*, writing to his mistress Sophie Volland: 'What a good use of genius! ... In the unlikely event that Christ exists, I can assure you that Voltaire will be saved.'

Chapter 8
The celebrity

The way in which we sum up Voltaire's achievement as a thinker and writer depends very much on how we understand the broader movement of ideas within which he was working, and as different views of the Age of Enlightenment have dominated at various times, so Voltaire's stock has risen or fallen. When the literary historian Daniel Mornet published an influential work on the intellectual origins of the French Revolution in 1933, he took it for granted that the 'critical spirit' of Voltaire and the other *philosophes* created a climate of opinion in the 1770s and 1780s which directly influenced the actors of the French Revolution. Since then, the picture has become more complex: the Enlightenment is no longer seen as a purely French phenomenon, or even as Franco-centric; meanwhile the French Revolution is contextualized alongside other revolutions in America and elsewhere.

Ideas of Enlightenment

Where does this leave Voltaire? A monarchist, broadly opposed to concepts of social and political equality, we do not look to him for statements of radical egalitarianism. Up until the mid-20th century, Voltaire was loved or loathed as a militant critic of the Catholic Church and the cheerleader of radical free-thinking. In 1956, the French academic René Pomeau published a book with what was then a provocative title: *La Religion de Voltaire* suggests that Voltaire's numerous protestations of deist belief should be taken at face value, a thesis which found broad (though not universal) acceptance in the second half of the 20th century. In recent years, the historian Jonathan Israel has written extensively on the Enlightenment, arguing for a distinction between what he calls the 'radical' Enlightenment, essentially the atheistic tradition deriving from Spinozan materialism, and the 'moderate' Enlightenment that embraces some minimalist notion of God, that went under the name of natural religion or deism. According to this divide, Voltaire emerges (as in Pomeau's thesis) as a 'moderate', someone who by implication doesn't dare to follow his ideas through to their logical conclusion and who therefore seems less interesting than his full-blooded radical contemporaries.

This criticism of Voltaire, if it is one, is all the more persuasive insofar as it was one levelled at him already in his own lifetime: Voltaire came at the end of his long life to be viewed as a somewhat antiquated figure; indeed he rather played up to the image, sporting old-fashioned court dress when he was fêted at the Comédie-Française just before his death. But then we should remember his love of acting: perhaps playing the role of an old-fashioned author, whose seemingly safe respectability offered cover for his radicalism, was just one last role he chose to try out?

The Enlightenment is typically viewed as a turning point in Western civilization because of its emphasis on secular values and on the study of man in the context of human society rather than from the perspective of his relationship to God. But it would be an error to think that Enlightened thinkers were automatically hostile to religion. Voltaire wrote about religion with what amounts to obsession: his earliest verse, as we have seen, is imbued with an Epicurean refusal of superstition and fear of the gods, and in his final years he composed a (highly partial)

Histoire de l'établissement du christianisme. Many of his polemical works are based on detailed knowledge of the Bible and biblical criticism, and when he was living in or near Geneva and needed to know more about the details of biblical teaching, his most learned interlocutors were some of the Genevan pastors with whom he corresponded. The opposition between atheism and deism (a defining distinction for Jonathan Israel) was perhaps not such a critical distinction in the 18th century, when thinkers, including believers, are often less interested in the metaphysics of revelation than in the practical concerns of defending freedom of belief in the interests of social peace and cohesion. For Voltaire, the greatest ills are the religious wars which have needlessly torn societies apart, and he returns time and again to the example of the French wars of religion, in particular the St Bartholomew's Day massacre: it is attested that he became sick every year on the anniversary of that bloody event.

Put another way, Voltaire's interest in religion was essentially historical: he wanted to demonstrate, with the forensic skills of the historian, that aspects of the biblical narrative were illogical, inconsistent, irrational, unworthy of our unconditional belief: why would we persecute our fellow man on the basis of such flimsy and contradictory evidence? This historical enquiry into the nature of religion, as part of a broader concern with the progress of knowledge, puts Voltaire at the heart of the Enlightenment endeavour. John Robertson sees a desire to better the human condition as the overriding theme uniting Enlightened thinkers in different parts of Europe, and he defines the Enlightenment as 'a distinct intellectual movement of the eighteenth century, dedicated to the better understanding, and thence the practical advancement, of the human condition on this earth'.

By this definition, with its emphasis on 'practical advancement', Voltaire is certainly a significant actor in the movement we now call the Enlightenment. Dennis Rasmussen, in a recent attempt to present Enlightenment thinking as the forerunner of modern liberalism, replaces Jonathan Israel's dichotomy of radical and moderate Enlightenments with the idea of the 'pragmatic Enlightenment', where the practically minded political thinkers like Voltaire and Montesquieu in France, Hume and Adam Smith in Britain, are opposed to the more idealistic thinkers who came up with more abstract theories. In a much-quoted phrase, in which Voltaire compares himself with Jean-Jacques Rousseau, he declares that 'I write to act; he writes for the sake of writing.' If we take this idea of 'writing to take action' as the key to understanding Voltaire, the question then becomes 'how?' It is not sufficient to examine his ideas in isolation if we wish to understand their true importance: we need to understand the way in which they were communicated so as to reach their public most vividly and most efficiently. Voltaire is a radical, but his radical Enlightenment is not of the sort described by Jonathan Israel; and to understand that, we need to appreciate Voltaire's style of authorship and its relationship to celebrity.

Public sphere

In recent years there has been much discussion about how Enlightenment ideas spread following the emergence of the 'public sphere'. The expression comes from Jürgen Habermas's *The Structural Transformation of the Public Sphere*, first published in German in 1962, which provoked considerable debate, especially after the appearance of an English translation in 1989. An example of the public sphere in action would be the coffee-house, as a space where citizens could freely gather to discuss public affairs. Addison, in the first issue of the *Spectator* (1711), explains how he gathers his information: 'I appear on Sunday nights at St James coffee house and sometimes join the little committee of politics in the inner room.' What Addison is describing here is not just a new source of information but in effect a new reading public: the *Spectator*—and we should remember that Voltaire learned English by reading the *Spectator*—addressed its readership on a range of matters of public interest in a language that was unstuffy, familiar, often slightly ironical. The possibilities offered by this literary and linguistic model for Voltaire are obvious.

The Parisian salons of the 18th century, much idealized in the 19th as the epitome of wit and sophistication, have been seen as another focus for writers to exchange views away from the watchful eye of government. The historian Antoine Lilti has recently questioned this view, showing that the salons in fact provided a sociable space in which men and women of letters mixed with aristocrats, so providing writers with access to power and influence. Voltaire of course lived most of his life away from the capital so did not frequent the Parisian salons, but he was able to maintain his profile in the capital with his correspondence and it was the sociability of the salons that allowed him to develop his correspondence networks.

This is most obviously the case with his exchanges with the marquise Du Deffand, whom he had known since the 1720s and with whom he exchanged frequent letters in the 1760s and 1770s. Mme Du Deffand was on intimate terms with the duchesse de Luxembourg, the prince de Conti, and the duc and duchesse de Choiseul, and Voltaire could be assured that a letter to Mme Du Deffand would be read aloud and shared with the other members of her elite society. She replied to one of Voltaire's letters saying, 'Your letter is charming—everyone asked me for copies of it.' Letters might have been copied, by certain privileged and approved individuals, but it would have been a gross breach of unwritten protocol to have printed a letter to which one had gained access in these circumstances. Voltaire is thus able to use his correspondence to influence those in positions of power, fully aware that his letters circulate in a network operating in what one might call a semi-public sphere.

Print trade

To reach a broader public, Voltaire of course used the medium of publishing. Eighteenth-century print culture was dynamic and ideas could circulate in books, brochures, and newspapers, and also as printed images. Compared with the previous century, levels of literacy were higher across western Europe and the burgeoning number of printers made available cheap books in smaller duodecimo formats—the equivalent of modern paperbacks. On the other hand, censorship in some form existed in most European countries; in France, books could be censored by the Church or by the *parlements* as well as by the government, which ran an office to control the book trade.

Voltaire understood better than anyone how to manipulate the book trade. To begin with, he was interested in the practicalities of printing and his surviving letters to various printers contain precise instructions concerning the width of margins, the typeface, the running heads, which show his understanding of the printer's craft. As he wrote to one correspondent, 'you don't print a book the way you sell cod in the market'. He was also extremely astute in his dealings with printers (the distinction between printer and publisher is not clear in the 18th century) to ensure the widest circulation of his works. This was a period when authors could make money out of a best-seller, but Voltaire quickly became sufficiently wealthy not to have to worry about earning money from his books: his concern was always to publish his books, circumventing the censor if necessary, so as to communicate his message. So in the early 1770s, when Voltaire published the *Questions sur l'Encyclopédie* with his regular printer Cramer in Geneva, he supplied behind Cramer's back a copy of the proofs, somewhat expanded, to another publisher in Neuchâtel. Books by Voltaire were likely to sell well, and by creating competition between two rival printers, he was both ensuring maximum saturation of the market and guaranteeing the continuing availability of his work in the event that the police in one state seized a printer's stock.

Censorship was an evident problem and Voltaire would never forget that he came close to being jailed following the publication of the *Letters on the English*. As he became more assured in his handling of the book trade, he became ever more resourceful in the marketing of his authorship. Today we take it for granted that an author puts his name on the title page, but this practice was far from standard in the 18th century. Voltaire will habitually sign plays or works of history, but in other cases he often publishes anonymously or with a fanciful pseudonym ('the archbishop of Novgorod'). Such is his fame, and so recognizable is his voice, that he doesn't need to sign his books—everyone knows anyway. The advantage of not signing was obvious: if the police took an interest in suppressing some heterodox work, Voltaire could always deny his authorship and it would be up to the police to prove he was lying. And his genius is to turn everything into a game: 'God preserve me, my dear brother, from having anything to do with the *Pocket Philosophical Dictionary*! I have read some of it: it reeks horribly of heresy,' wrote Voltaire to his reliable friend Damilaville in Paris. Then he added, 'But since you are curious about these irreligious works and keen to refute them, I'll look out a few copies, and send them to you at the first opportunity.' Thus in the same letter, Voltaire promises his close collaborator copies of the new work banned in Paris, while also providing him with a sentence or two which could be read out to interested parties at opportune moments. The trick was to confuse the opposition. To different correspondents Voltaire writes that he is not the author of the *Dictionnaire*, or that it is by some student called 'Dubut', or yet again that this is a collective work written by several authors. No one needed to believe any of this, but it created enough false trails to wrong-foot the censors, a game in which Voltaire revelled.

The more famous Voltaire became, the more remarkable was the impact of his writings. In September 1770, the king of Denmark, Christian VII, declared the freedom of the press in all his territories. This was an extraordinary moment in the history of the Enlightenment, the first time that any country had officially made such a declaration. The 76-year-old Voltaire sprang into action, writing an *Épître au roi de Danemark*. The poem lavishes extravagant praise on the Danish king—Voltaire declares implausibly that the one consolation of his life would be to become a Danish subject—before attacking the lack of press freedom in France: 'Sans l'agrément du roi vous ne pouvez penser | Pour avoir de l'esprit allez à la police' ('You cannot think without the king's pleasure, If you wish to be witty, go to the police'). There is a clear Enlightenment message here: Voltaire is holding up the decision of the king of Denmark—soon to be rescinded, but that's another story, told in the film *A Royal Affair*—as a model for other crowned heads of Europe, beginning with Louis XV.

What is interesting here is not so much the poem itself (which is competent but no more) but rather the mechanism by which Voltaire publicized it. In late 1770, he teasingly tells D'Alembert in Paris about the new poem, but doesn't send it to him. On 15 January 1771 Voltaire sends the poem in manuscript to Christian VII (and the ten-page manuscript is still to be found today in the Royal Library in Copenhagen). Then Voltaire tells other highly placed friends in Paris about the poem (the comte d'Argental, the duchesse de Choiseul), praising the Danish king's example, complaining about the lack of press liberty in France, but still not passing on the actual poem. He builds up an appetite for his new work, claiming implausibly that he has difficulty making copies, or playfully pretending that he dare not show the work to certain correspondents because of its contents. This flirtation is carried on even with Catherine the Great: Voltaire tells her that she is mentioned in his epistle to the king of Denmark, but that he won't send her the poem unless she asks for it, which of course she does, instantly, Catherine being as keen on good publicity as Voltaire.

Eventually Voltaire posts the poem in manuscript to D'Alembert, on 2 March 1771, several months after first promising it. He urges his friend to show caution and not allow copies to be made: 'I tremble at the thought of this work getting spread around.' As expected, multiple manuscript copies circulate instantly around Paris, so that by 11 March the poem is referred to in a journal and on 1 April it is printed in the *Journal encyclopédique* (and thereafter in various collections of Voltaire's writings). In Denmark, meanwhile, the king immediately arranged for the Voltaire poem to be printed in Copenhagen, first in French and then in Danish translation—this was useful publicity for him too. The publication of the *Épître au roi de Danemark* is an object lesson in how to achieve maximum publicity for a publication with minimum effort: the success of the operation depended crucially on Voltaire's celebrity.

Celebrity culture

Modern celebrity culture has its origins in the 18th century, 'an age', as Leo Braudy puts it, 'preoccupied with the question of self-definition in public'. Certain individuals including writers might enjoy a reputation within their peer group, but celebrity was different, because it reached out far beyond Habermas's public sphere, more widely and more indiscriminately. As the aphorist Chamfort put it: 'Celebrity is the advantage of being known to people who don't know you.' Celebrity culture emerged when economic conditions in major urban centres like Paris and London had created a public of consumers, while at the same time there was a new emphasis on privacy and intimacy: suddenly there was a public fascinated by the private lives of famous people and clamouring for at least the pretence of intimacy with them.

Voltaire manages the critical transition from being a famous writer to being a celebrity writer, perhaps, as Lilti has recently suggested, the first celebrity writer in European culture. The patriarch of Ferney had become a star and people would write to him on any pretext, simply to oblige him to write back, so that they would have a note in the hand of the great man—today, we'd call them autograph hunters. Huber, the Genevan artist, depicted Voltaire pulling on his trousers while he dictated to his secretary: this painting, *Le Lever de Voltaire* (1772), became the basis of a number of engravings which sold widely in France and beyond. Traditionally, a great writer would have been portrayed in a thoughtful pose, perhaps holding a pen; now a new public wants to see Voltaire with his trousers (almost) down, the great man being glimpsed in the (pretend) intimacy of his bedroom. Voltaire claimed to disapprove, but of course he must have connived with Huber in the production of the painting. Even so, celebrity was a hard thing to manage and the multiplication of cheap prints, once it began, was out of his control. Some of the prints appeared with flattering verses underneath, other prints of the same image were published with verses critical of Voltaire. But his celebrity was not dented and Voltaire understood the need to remain always in the public eye.

A celebrity writer didn't just have to be famous for his books, he (rarely she) could be famous for being famous. An example of the publicity machine in action is an article that appeared in Grimm's *Correspondance littéraire* in 1769, describing how Catherine the Great had sent two Russian officers to the château de Ferney, bearing gifts for Voltaire: an ivory box, turned by the empress herself, containing her portrait; a magnificent fur; and a selection of her writings, including the *Nakaz*, her statement of enlightened legal principles proclaiming the equality of all before the law and her rejection of torture. 'It is said,' the article goes on, 'that the Imperial embassy has rejuvenated the Patriarch by ten years.' This is a wonderful Enlightenment morality tale, as politically helpful to Voltaire as it is to Catherine. But where did Grimm find his information? It is possible that the two Russian officers supplied him with an account, but that seems improbable. Voltaire was in regular touch with Grimm, who published in his journal a regular supplement of Voltaire's letters, so it seems most likely that the flattering account was supplied by Voltaire himself.

Of all the thinkers of the 18th century, it was surely Voltaire who was the most media-savvy. His celebrity status meant that his books, and his message, reached ever wider audiences. Critics have sometimes said that Voltaire's thought does not develop, even that he repeats himself in his later works—this is true, as Voltaire himself was the first to admit: 'I shall repeat here what I've already said elsewhere, and what must go on being repeated until such time as the French understand…'. But perhaps, when considering his significance as a thinker, we should pay more attention to the size and breadth of his readership, and the fact that his celebrity status carried his message to ever greater numbers. Voltaire's importance can be measured not only by the originality or importance of his ideas, but by the number of people he influenced.

Voltaire, always the actor, kept up the performance to the end. In 1778 the 84-year-old returned to Paris after an absence of twenty-eight years. His health was increasingly fragile and he died there on 30 May. A few months beforehand, he had been specially honoured by the Comédie-Française, when he attended a performance of his last tragedy, *Irène*. At the end of the play, Voltaire's bust was placed on stage, the actress Madame Vestris read verses specially composed for the occasion by M. de Saint-Marc, and the performers then came in turn to place wreaths on the bust. According to all accounts the theatre was in a frenzy and this spread out into the streets as Voltaire made his journey home. Here is how the popular actor Fleury later recalled (or rather re-imagined) the scene in his memoirs:

As his carriage was turning by the rue du Bac, a crowd of bare-armed workmen came out of their workshop to see the procession.

I confess they didn't seem to fully appreciate his standing as a writer. For them, Voltaire was a philosopher, that is to say, in their minds, an enemy of priests...They ran after him, rushing at his carriage, throwing their hats in the air, crying out, amidst all the other cries: 'Long live the defender of Calas! Long live the defender of Sirven!'...Fanaticism and intolerance dared show themselves only in secret, and perhaps for the first time in France, we saw public opinion assume fully its proper place.

'Voltaire expresses [fame]', writes Leo Braudy, 'by choosing to live like an aristocrat of old, constantly in a crowd, casting his entourage in plays of his own devising, onstage and off.' Voltaire had always been an instinctive performer and it was fitting that this, his farewell performance, should take place in the theatre. The events were widely reported in newspapers and the artist Jean-Michel Moreau recorded the scene in a drawing that was engraved and widely distributed. Voltaire's coronation at the Comédie-Française had become a public event.

Chapter 9
The life and the afterlife

The vogue for biographies of Voltaire seems unstoppable, yet it is no easy matter to write a satisfactory account of his life: we know too much and too little. Too much, because faced by such a long life and such an intimidating output—some 200 volumes in the new Oxford edition—it is difficult to produce a comprehensive view of this writer that does not lose itself in detail. Too little, because so much of the evidence is problematic. Any biographer must rely heavily on Voltaire's own words, in particular his correspondence, which is extensive and irresistible. Yet we know Voltaire's preoccupation with creating Voltaire, so we are wary of relying on his own words and we look for other documentary evidence, descriptions, anecdotes, or images. And the more we look, the more we realize that even this evidence is often contaminated: so often Voltaire planted the anecdotes we use to describe him, just as he shaped and controlled the images of himself that circulated. He became increasingly adept at shaping the way posterity would judge him, and his creative input into the evidence of his life becomes the story of his life. It is interesting that no one has ever written a biography of François-Marie Arouet (and what might that look like?). We talk instead about the author invented by Arouet and this book has tried to tell the story of that invention. In fact, Voltaire was not one but a series of inventions and reinventions, a series of authorial postures or stances, by which 'Voltaire' adapted himself as circumstances necessitated. The

19th-century French critic Ferdinand Brunetière speaks more truly than he knows when he writes that 'perhaps, in the end, Voltaire's masterpiece is his life'.

The French Revolution

Another challenge is the long shadow cast by Voltaire's reputation. For a writer who didn't believe in life after death, his afterlife on earth has been spectacularly rich—and contradictory. Historians of ideas speculate about the extent to which he and his fellow *philosophes* prepared the ground for the French Revolution; the critic Gustave Lanson went so far as to describe the *Letters on the English* as 'the first bomb thrown at the Ancien Régime'. But we might also turn the question round: to what extent did the Revolution of 1789 interrupt and derail the ideas of the (late) Enlightenment? On several occasions in his letters Voltaire looks forward with approval to the 'revolution' to come—and he emphatically does not mean the Revolution with a capital 'R'; he has in mind a forthcoming 'revolution' in ideas when man will finally free himself from the influence of established religion(s), cast off the shackles of prejudice and superstition, and learn to think for himself.

The Revolution was to change radically the popular image of Voltaire. The National Constituent Assembly resolved to convert the newly built neoclassical church in Paris's Latin Quarter into the Panthéon, a mausoleum for great men (the first 'great woman' was Marie Curie in 1995). Voltaire was the first writer to be so honoured (Jean-Jacques Rousseau would follow two years later) and, in July 1791, Voltaire's mortal remains—minus the brain and heart, which had been removed—were transferred to their new resting place in a long procession which was remembered as one of the Revolution's great public ceremonies. The hearse made its way first to the Place de la Bastille and the crowd watched as the coffin was placed on a highly symbolic pile of rubble, the stones of the Bastille prison. The next day, after the rain had stopped, the procession which set off across Paris to the Panthéon included soldiers as well as actors and students, a model of the Bastille, a statue of the great man, even a set of his complete writings in seventy volumes—this was a secular version of a religious procession, even to the inclusion of resting places resembling stations of the cross. On the coffin was an inscription reclaiming Voltaire as a hero of the Revolution: 'He avenged Calas, La Barre, Sirven and Monbailli. Poet, philosopher, historian, he made the human mind soar and prepared us to be free.'

The 19th century

Never mind that Voltaire was a monarchist, a bourgeois who believed in finding an accommodation with the powers that be, a writer who at various times had used his correspondence to lend moral authority to the causes of Frederick the Great or Catherine II; never mind, above all, that Voltaire throughout his life had battled to ridicule the harmful excesses of fanatical enthusiasm and that he would unquestionably have rejected the Revolutionaries out of hand. Voltaire, a casualty perhaps of his own celebrity, had become an iconic figure for the French Revolution and this image was to stick with him for the next two centuries. France in the 19th century underwent a series of political upheavals, as the tension between monarchists and republicans continued, and in the new political divide between 'Left' and 'Right', the name of Voltaire was inevitably associated with the Left, just as the defence of the Catholic Church was naturally part of the programme of the Right. Whenever the state and the Church were under particular attack, it was always the name of Voltaire that came to the fore. The Dreyfus affair in the 1890s, when a Jewish French officer was unjustly found guilty of treason, provoked a national schism between Dreyfusards and anti-Dreyfusards, and many drew parallels between the campaign to defend Dreyfus and that to defend Calas in the 1760s.

In the eyes of some, Voltaire was a political hero, the model of how a writer can take a stand on issues of public interest, and both Victor Hugo, who campaigned against the death penalty, and Émile Zola, who defended Dreyfus in the press (beginning with the famous article 'J'accuse'), considered themselves to be successors to Voltaire. Some authors of the 19th century, forgetting that Voltaire was a master of irony, chose to caricature him as a dry rationalist lacking in poetic soul. It didn't help that Voltaire had said of himself that 'I am like those small streams that are clear because they are shallow'. For the modernist poet Baudelaire, Voltaire epitomized the boring bourgeoisie; in his *Mon cœur mis à nu*, he describes Voltaire as the 'anti-poet', the 'prince of the superficial', and, worst of all, a 'preacher for concierges'. The prominent French critic Émile Faguet famously referred to Voltaire's thinking as 'a chaos of clear ideas', while the philosopher Victor Cousin spoke cuttingly of Voltaire's 'common sense, universal and superficial'. The novelist Flaubert, who venerated Voltaire as a stylist, rivalled him in his complex use of irony. In *Madame Bovary*, the self-satisfied and narrow-minded pharmacist Homais is proud to style himself a 'Voltairean', while in his *Dictionnaire des idées reçues*, Flaubert pokes fun at the bourgeois who trot out the cliché of Voltaire's 'superficial learning'. Nietzsche's was a lone voice in his century when he acclaimed Voltaire as the last free spirit.

Others attacked Voltaire with venom. In the eyes of the Catholic Church in the 19th century, he became a hate figure; already in the 18th century, he had been represented as the Antichrist and the personification now became frequent. A lithograph by the great caricaturist Honoré Daumier, published in *Le Charivari* on 22 September 1869, sums up the hostility between Voltaire and (parts of) the Church: a seated Voltaire (reminiscent of Houdon's famous statue) looks on smiling at a furious Jesuit who has ink dripping from his hands: 'I wanted to throw the ink at *him*, but I'm the one who has got dirty' runs the caption (see Figure 9). Daumier was an anticlerical and militant Republican; the Jesuits, expelled from

Je voulais la lui jeter et c'est moi qui me suis sali.

9. 'I wanted to throw the ink at _him_, but I'm the one who has got dirty'. Cartoon by Honoré Daumier, published in _Le Charivari_, 22 September 1869.

France in 1762, had returned in 1865, and it is natural that it should be Voltaire who represents the forces of opposition to the Church.

Modern reactions

Many books have been written by pious Christians defaming Voltaire, some of them launching myths that survive to this day—for example the idea that Voltaire enriched himself from the slave trade. It is true that he held views on race that are far from 'enlightened' in the modern sense. Against the Christian monogenetic belief that the whole human race was descended from a single pair, Adam and Eve, Voltaire (like David Hume) defended polygenesis, the view that human races are of different origins—a position which has often been (though it need not be) connected with the defence of slavery and the notion of 'inferior' races. It is certainly the case that Voltaire held investments in the French India Company which traded in many different goods, including slaves, but serious scholars in the 20th century have gone further by stating incontrovertibly that Voltaire made himself rich by investing in the slave trade. This story, it turns out, derives from a book of the 1870s which cites a letter in which Voltaire gloats over his gains from the slave trade: the book in question is a denunciation of Voltaire written from a militantly Catholic standpoint and the letter quoted is in fact entirely spurious. Voltaire was not prominent in attacking slavery—the campaign for abolition gained momentum only in the 1780s, after his death—but he did not deliberately profit from the slave trade either.

More complex to refute is the argument that Voltaire was anti-Semitic, a charge that continues to be levelled with great frequency. Voltaire has many of the prejudices of his day and says many things (about Jews, women, gays...) that make modern liberals uncomfortable; more to the point, he has a particular obsession with Jewish history, because he wants to remind complacent Christians that the history of the world cannot and should not be reduced to the history of the Jewish people as recounted in the Old Testament. But Voltaire was unrelenting in defending all those, Jews included, who were the object of religious persecution, and he had an abiding disgust—the word is not too strong—for the way politicians seek power by cynically exploiting the religious credulity of the populace: these themes have strong modern resonance, and it seems misplaced to characterize Voltaire as anti-Semitic in the way that the word, post-Holocaust, is now employed. Those who have argued differently have often relied, openly or not, on a work of pro-Nazi propaganda by Henri Labroue; his book is widely available on the web, though the online editions omit to say that it was published in France in 1942, during the German occupation. After the Liberation of Paris, in August 1944, the French poet Jean Tardieu adapted *Candide* as a radio play that was first broadcast in December that year. Voltaire's is a name that all sides sought to appropriate.

Whatever the political climate, however, Voltaire has always had his readers—one advantage of writing so much and in so many different literary forms is that there is something for all tastes and all times. Many in the 19th century were wary of his reputation for being irreligious, but they still read his epic poem *La Henriade* and went to see his tragedies performed at the theatre. His history of the reign of Louis XIV was pleasing to the most ardent monarchist and the work acquired the status of a classic, reprinted regularly all through the century. Voltairean values came truly to the fore during the Third Republic, created in 1870 in the wake of the collapse of the Second Empire following the Prussian invasion.

The young republic introduced widespread educational reforms and Voltaire made his appearance on university syllabuses from the 1890s. The formal separation of Church and state in 1905 was a fundamentally Voltairean gesture, enshrining in law the principle of a secular state. It was around this time that the leading critic of the day, Gustave Lanson, produced the first modern edition of the *Lettres philosophiques*, coinciding more or less with the *entente cordiale* that was uniting Britain and France at a time when war against Germany seemed increasingly likely. The *Letters on the English*, a work forgotten since the 18th century, suddenly featured on school and university syllabuses on both sides of the Channel and has remained widely studied ever since. By the time of the First World War, the *Siècle de Louis XIV* had been overtaken by the work of more 'modern' historians like Ernest Lavisse, but if Voltaire's work as a historian now appeared dated and his poetry and theatre was becoming neglected, it was Voltaire the writer of fiction who came to the fore in the course of the 20th century, and his philosophical tales are now republished and retranslated endlessly—a development that would surely have mystified Voltaire himself.

The potency of Voltaire's legacy is felt far beyond France and has become a defining strand of Western culture: when the young Leonard Woolf, fresh from Cambridge, joined the Ceylon Civil Service before the First World War, he took with him the complete works of Voltaire in seventy volumes (see Box 7). Whenever intellectuals wish to hold tight to Enlightenment values, it is to Voltaire they turn. In the late 1930s, with Europe on the brink of war, W. H. Auden evokes the patriarch of Ferney as a symbol of the writer's fight against persecution and stupidity. In his poem 'Voltaire at Ferney', dated February 1939, the figure of Voltaire stands watch over Europe, his pen the last remaining defence against the horrors in store: 'Yes, like a sentinel, he could

Box 7 Voltaire as cultural baggage

I had some liabilities and three assets, when I arrived in M—. One of the liabilities was the 70 large volumes of Voltaire printed in Paris in 1784, which socially and psychologically did me no good and materially throughout my six years in India proved a considerable difficulty when they had to be moved over hundreds of miles in a country without railways. I am rather proud of the fact that socially I lived down the 70 volumes and physically brought them back to England in fair conditions neither repudiating Voltaire spiritually and socially nor abandoning him materially.

(Leonard Woolf, *Memoirs of an Elderly Man*, 1945)

not sleep. The night was full of wrong...' Later, during the war in Vietnam, when De Gaulle was asked why he had not had Sartre arrested for his anti-war protests, the French President is said to have replied, 'you can't arrest Voltaire'. Many modern satirists have learned their trade from Voltaire. The caustic black humour of the film *Dr Strangelove* (1964)—full title, *Dr Strangelove, or How I learned to stop worrying and love the bomb*—bears a distinctly Voltairean imprint, not surprisingly since Terry Southern, one of its co-writers, had earlier co-authored the novel *Candy* (1958), a provocative reworking of *Candide*, later turned into a film (1968).

Voltaire's legacy is more than a body of thought or a number of great books (important though they are). More than these things, Voltaire has left us with a voice, a tool for debunking self-important authority with scepticism and irony, and this tool has lost none of its potency. It is Voltaire's voice we hear loud and clear when Woody Allen (in the film *Love and Death*) explains that 'If it turns out there is a God, I don't think He is evil. I think that the worst thing that you can say about Him is that He is an underachiever.' Or to paraphrase Voltaire's much quoted dictum about God, if Voltaire hadn't existed, we would have had to invent him.

Our debt to Voltaire in current debates about religious toleration and free speech is all too evident. Hardly a week passes without an article in the press quoting Voltaire and in particular 'I disapprove of what you say, but I will defend to the death your right to say it.' This rallying cry of free speech is so potent that it seems pedantic to point out that Voltaire never actually said it. It so happens that the expression was made up in 1906 by an English woman biographer, E. B. Hall. No matter—it expresses a truth which is authentically Voltairean and fundamentally important to our culture, so we have adopted the phrase and decided that Voltaire should have said it. Another dictum which has recently gained wide currency on the Internet is 'To learn who rules over you,

simply find out who you are not allowed to criticize': regularly
attributed to Voltaire, the saying apparently derives from
something written in 1993 by an American neo-Nazi Holocaust
denier, Kevin Alfred Strom. The Voltaire name remains a potent
source of authority—and not only among liberals.

10. Photo taken on Boulevard Voltaire, Paris, 10 January 2015,
following the terrorist attacks in that city.

After the *Charlie Hebdo* killings in Paris in January 2015, when the slogan 'Je suis Charlie' appeared widely in the media, a poster showing Voltaire saying 'Je suis Charlie' appeared on the walls in Paris (see Figure 10). Large numbers attended a rally to express sympathy with the victims and outrage at this attack on the secular values of the republic: they marched down the Boulevard Voltaire to congregate in the Place de la Bastille (two of the most emblematic names in French republican history). The following day the leading cartoonist Plantu featured the rally in his cartoon on the front page of *Le Monde*: the marchers walk down the Boulevard Voltaire brandishing their pencils, while looking on from above, three Muslims, who appear to be boiling in hell, are asking 'C'est qui Voltaire?', 'Who is this Voltaire?' (see Figure 11).

Voltaire's name is synonymous with a set of values that transcend his writing: dislike of bigotry and superstition, belief in reason and toleration, freedom of speech. He has been a model for other

11. 'Who is this Voltaire?' Cartoon by Plantu, *Le Monde*, 12 January 2015.

Box 8 G. B. Shaw on Voltaire's legacy

Everybody now sees that Voltaire did a great service to religion by winning the right to criticize and question the authority of the Church as if it were no more sacred than any other human institution. Yet he did this service by shocking the world with lampoons upon the most sacred subjects—lampoons which were chaste in comparison to the rhapsodies in many books of devotion, but which, to the prejudices of his contemporaries, were beyond measure indecorous and scandalous. These lampoons did not, as shallow people feared, destroy religion and corrupt the world: nobody reads them now; but they secured the right of discussion which many great thinkers immediately availed themselves of to let light into dark places and fresh air into unwholesome sanctuaries.

(George Bernard Shaw, 1889)

great writers, like George Bernard Shaw, who have adapted these values to the struggles of their own day (see Box 8). This is a potent legacy, but not a static one. In the proper spirit of the Enlightenment, we continue to dialogue with Voltaire and in so doing we perpetuate his legacy.

A chronology of Voltaire's life and works

1694	Born François-Marie Arouet, in Paris.
1704–11	Pupil at the Jesuit college Louis-le-Grand, the most famous school in Paris.
1713	First journey abroad, to The Hague.
1716	Exiled from Paris because of a satire against the Regent.
1718	Adopts the name Voltaire. His tragedy *Œdipe* is staged at the Comédie-Française with great success.
1723	French government refuses to allow publication of *La Ligue* (later called *La Henriade*).
1726–8	Voltaire lives in London, learns English, and meets English writers.
1728	Publishes *La Henriade* in French, in London, dedicated to Queen Caroline.
1733	*Letters Concerning the English Nation* published in London.
1734	A French version of the *Letters Concerning the English Nation*, entitled *Lettres philosophiques*, published in Rouen and immediately censored.
1734–49	Settles at Cirey (in Champagne) with his companion Émilie Du Châtelet. They share a period of intense literary and scientific activity.
1736	Publishes *Le Mondain*, a poem about luxury.
1743	Elected a Fellow of the Royal Society.

1745	Enjoys a brief period of favour at court. Appointed Historiographer of France by Louis XV. Writes two opera libretti, *La Princesse de Navarre* and *Le Temple de la gloire*, set to music by Rameau.
1746	Elected to the Académie française. Begins a liaison with his niece, Mme Denis.
1749	Émilie Du Châtelet dies. Voltaire leaves Cirey and returns to Paris.
1750-3	At the court of Frederick the Great in Berlin and Potsdam.
1751	The *Siècle de Louis XIV* is published in Berlin.
1753	Voltaire quarrels with Frederick and leaves his court.
1755-9	Lives in Geneva, in a house called 'Les Délices' (now the Musée Voltaire).
1755	Lisbon earthquake; news reaches Voltaire in late November.
1756	Publishes the *Poème sur le désastre de Lisbonne* and the first official edition of the *Essai sur les mœurs*, a pioneering global history.
1759	*Candide* appears in Geneva; sixteen other editions appear across Europe.
1759-78	Voltaire lives in the château de Ferney, in France, close to Geneva. He is celebrated across Europe as the 'patriarch of Ferney'.
1760	First use of the catch phrase *Écrasez l'infâme* ('Crush the despicable') that epitomizes his crusade for religious toleration.
1762	Large edition of Voltaire's writings appears in English translation (by Smollett and Francklin). Voltaire begins campaign to rehabilitate the memory of the Protestant Jean Calas, unjustly condemned for the murder of his son.
1763	Publishes the *Traité sur la tolérance*.
1764	Publishes the *Dictionnaire philosophique portatif*. Enlarged editions continue to appear until 1769.
1770-2	Publishes the *Questions sur l'Encyclopédie*, his last alphabetical collection of articles.

| 1778 | Returns to Paris for the first time in twenty-eight years. Attends a meeting of the Académie française, is fêted at the Comédie-Française, and dies soon after. |
| 1791 | In one of the great Revolutionary celebrations, Voltaire's mortal remains are carried in procession through Paris and transferred to the Panthéon, where they remain today. |

References

All translations from French unless otherwise stated are my own.

Introduction

Jorge Luis Borges and Osvaldo Ferrari, *Conversations*, vol. 2 (London: Seagull Books, 2015), 'Voltaire', pp. 220–6 (p. 221).

Pietro Verri: letter to his brother Alessandro, 3 January 1769.

'The best effect of a book is to make men think': Voltaire, *Panégyrique de Louis XV*.

Chapter 1: The man of theatre

Voltaire as actor: R. S. Ridgway, 'Voltaire as an Actor', *Eighteenth-Century Studies*, 1 (1968), pp. 261–76.

Lekain in Dijon: Lauren R. Clay, *Stagestruck: The Business of Theater in Eighteenth-Century France and its Colonies* (Ithaca, NY: Cornell University Press, 2013), p. 153.

Casanova in Lausanne: Casanova, *Histoire de ma vie*, vol. 6, ch. 9.

'Civilize Europe': Rahul Markovits, *Civiliser l'Europe: politiques du théâtre français au XVIIIᵉ siècle* (Paris: Fayard, 2014).

John Moore: quoted in Sir Gavin de Beer and André-Michel Rousseau, *Voltaire's British Visitors* (Oxford: Voltaire Foundation, 1967), pp. 165–6.

Caroline Lennox: letter dated 24 May 1767, quoted in James T. Boulton and T. O. McLoughlin (eds), *News from Abroad: Letters Written by British Travellers on the Grand Tour, 1728–71* (Liverpool: Liverpool University Press, 2012), p. 258.

Chapter 2: The Epicurean poet

Nicholas Cronk, 'The Epicurean Spirit: Champagne and the Defence of Poetry in Voltaire's *Le Mondain*', *Studies on Voltaire and the Eighteenth Century*, 371 (1999), pp. 53–80.

Alan Charles Kors, *Epicureans and Atheists in France, 1650–1729* (Cambridge: Cambridge University Press, 2016).

Verses to Mme Du Châtelet: Richard Wilbur's translation first appeared separately in *The New York Review of Books* (18 June 1970); slightly revised, with the title 'To Madame du Châtelet', it was collected in his *The Mind-Reader* (New York: Harcourt Brace Jovanovich, 1976), pp. 38–9; the later version is quoted here. The Ezra Pound imitation is the second of a set of three 'Impressions of François-Marie Arouet (de Voltaire)' (1915–16), in *Personae: The Collected Poems of Ezra Pound* (New York: Liveright, 1926), pp. 167–8. Wilbur knew the imitation by Pound; and both poets were probably familiar with the translation of the *Verses to Mme Du Châtelet* by James Russell Lowell, first published in Henry Wadsworth Longfellow (ed.), *The Poets and Poetry of Europe* (1871), and later collected in Lowell's *Uncollected Poems* (1950).

Chapter 3: The Englishman

Letter to Earl Bathurst: Nicholas Cronk, 'La Correspondance de Voltaire dans les collections de la New York Public Library', *Revue d'histoire littéraire de la France*, 112 (2012), pp. 653–92 (p. 659).

Nicholas Cronk, 'The *Letters Concerning the English Nation* as an English Work: Reconsidering the Harcourt Brown Thesis', *Studies on Voltaire and the Eighteenth Century*, 9 (2001), pp. 226–39.

István Hont, *Jealousy of Trade: International Competition and the Nation-State in Historical Perspective* (Cambridge, Mass.: Harvard University Press, 2005).

Lytton Strachey: 'Voltaire and England' (1914), in *Books and Characters: French and English* (London: Chatto & Windus, 1922), p. 115.

Sir William Temple, *Observations upon the United Provinces of the Netherlands*, introduction by G. N. Clark (Cambridge: Cambridge University Press, 1932).

Norman L. Torrey, *Voltaire and the English Deists* (New Haven: Yale University Press, 1930).

Matthew Sharpe, 'Cicero, Voltaire, and the *Philosophes* in the French Enlightenment', in William H. F. Altman (ed.), *Brill's Companion to the Reception of Cicero* (Leiden: Brill, 2015), ch. 13.

Chapter 4: The scientist

On Voltaire's reading of Newton: J. B. Shank, *The Newton Wars and the Beginning of the French Enlightenment* (Chicago: Chicago University Press, 2008).

'These whole areas of enquiry…': William Barber: 'Voltaire and Natural Science: from Apples to Fossils', in M. Delon and C. Seth (eds), *Voltaire en Europe: Hommage à Christiane Mervaud* (Oxford: Voltaire Foundation, 2000), pp. 243–54 (p. 250).

'He knew how to doubt': *Éléments de la philosophie de Newton*, part I, ch. 6.

Chapter 5: The courtier

On opera libretti, see 'Recordings' listed in Further Reading.

Chapter 6: The Genevan

Candide in tweets: Alexander Aciman and Emmett Rensin, *Twitterature: The World's Greatest Books Retold through Twitter* (London: Penguin Books, 2009), pp. 30–1.

Chapter 7: The campaigner

Nicholas Cronk, 'Voltaire and the 1760s: The Rule of the Patriarch', in N. Cronk (ed.), *Voltaire and the 1760s: Essays for John Renwick* (Oxford: Voltaire Foundation, 2008), pp. 9–21.

'Voltaire finally became a Voltairean': Michel Delon, 'Comment Voltaire est devenu voltairien', *Revue des Deux Mondes*, April 2015, pp. 25–32.

Lynn Hunt, *Inventing Human Rights: A History* (New York: Norton, 2007).

'The successor of St Peter': *Traité sur la tolérance*, ch. 11.

'Now it is hard to see how…': *Traité sur la tolérance*, ch. 6.

Élisabeth Claverie, 'Procès, affaire, cause: Voltaire et l'innovation critique', *Politix*, 26 (1994), pp. 76–85.

Chapter 8: The celebrity

John Robertson, *The Enlightenment: A Very Short Introduction* (Oxford: Oxford University Press, 2015), p. 13.

Dennis C. Rasmussen, *The Pragmatic Enlightenment: Recovering the Liberalism of Hume, Smith, Montesquieu, and Voltaire* (Cambridge: Cambridge University Press, 2014).

Antoine Lilti, *The World of the Salons: Sociability and Worldliness in Eighteenth-Century Paris* (New York: Oxford University Press, 2015).

'I shall repeat here…': *Questions sur l'Encyclopédie*, article 'Cul' ('Arse', 1771).

'an age preoccupied…': Leo Braudy, *The Frenzy of Renown: Fame and its History* (New York: Vintage Books, 1997), p. 371. On this topic, see also Antoine Lilti, *Figures publiques: l'invention de la célébrité, 1750–1850* (Paris: Fayard, 2014).

'Voltaire expresses fame…': Braudy, *The Frenzy of Renown*, p. 372.

Chapter 9: The life and the afterlife

On Voltaire and his enemies, see Darrin M. McMahon, *Enemies of the Enlightenment: The French Counter-Enlightenment and the Making of Modernity* (New York: Oxford University Press, 2001).

On Voltaire's alleged involvement in the slave trade, see Christopher L. Miller, *The French Atlantic Triangle: Literature and Culture of the Slave Trade* (Durham, NC: Duke University Press, 2008), pp. 428–9. Concerning Voltaire's views on race, see Andrew S. Curran, *The Anatomy of Blackness: Science and Slavery in an Age of Enlightenment* (Baltimore: Johns Hopkins University Press, 2011), pp. 137–49.

Jean Tardieu: *Candide*, 'Adaptation radiophonique du roman de Voltaire', in *Une soirée en Provence, ou le mot et le cri* (Paris: Gallimard, 1975), pp. 161–205.

G. B. Shaw on Voltaire's legacy: Dan H. Laurence and Margot Peters (eds), 'Unpublished Shaw', *Shaw: The Annual of Bernard Shaw Studies*, 16 (1996), p. 31.

Further reading

Translations

Candide and Other Stories, trans. and ed. Roger Pearson (Oxford: Oxford University Press, 1990; new edn, 2006).

Micromégas and Other Stories, trans. Douglas Parmée (Richmond: Alma Classics, 2014).

Candide, Norton Critical Edition, 3rd edn, trans. Robert M. Adams, ed. Nicholas Cronk (New York: Norton, 2016) [Contains essays on Voltaire and *Candide*].

Candide (Peterborough, Ont.: Broadview, 2009), ed. Eric Palmer; reproduces the translation published by John Nourse in London in 1759, *Candide, or All for the Best*.

Letters Concerning the English Nation, ed. Nicholas Cronk (Oxford: Oxford University Press, 1994; rev. edn, 2005) [Critical edition of the translation by John Lockman, published in London (1733) in advance of the French *Lettres philosophiques* (1734)].

A Pocket Philosophical Dictionary, trans. John Fletcher, ed. Nicholas Cronk, Oxford World's Classics (Oxford: Oxford University Press, 2011).

God and Human Beings, trans. Michael Shreve, ed. S. T. Joshi (Amherst, NY: Prometheus Books, 2010).

Political Writings, trans. David Williams (Cambridge: Cambridge University Press, 1994).

Select Letters of Voltaire, trans. Theodore Besterman (London: Nelson, 1963).

Treatise on Tolerance and Other Texts, trans. Brian Masters and Simon
  Harvey (Cambridge: Cambridge University Press, 2000).
Treatise on Toleration, trans. Desmond M. Clarke (London: Penguin,
  2016).
*Voltaire's Revolution: Writings from his Campaign to Free Laws from
  Religion*, trans. and ed. G. K. Noyer (Amherst, NY: Prometheus
  Books, 2015).
The Works of Voltaire (London, 1761–5), 35 volumes, ed. Tobias
  Smollett and Thomas Francklin; these volumes exist in modern
  reprints and can be found online.

Lives

Haydn Mason, *Voltaire: A Biography* (London: Granada, 1981).
Nancy Mitford, *Voltaire in Love*, introduction by Adam Gopnik
  (New York: NYRB, 2012).
Roger Pearson, *Voltaire Almighty: A Life in the Pursuit of Freedom*
  (London: Bloomsbury, 2005).

The Enlightenment context

W. H. Barber, *Leibniz in France from Arnauld to Voltaire: A Study in
  the French Reactions to Leibnizianism, 1670–1770* (Oxford:
  Clarendon Press, 1955).
Durand Echeverria, *The Maupeou Revolution: A Study in the History
  of Libertarianism: France, 1770–1774* (Baton Rouge: Louisiana
  State University Press, 1985).
Dan Edelstein, *The Enlightenment: A Genealogy* (Chicago: University
  of Chicago Press, 2010).
Vincenzo Ferrone, *The Enlightenment: History of an Idea* (Princeton:
  Princeton University Press, 2015).
Norman Hampson, *The Enlightenment* (Harmondsworth: Penguin,
  1968).
Paul Hazard, *The Crisis of the European Mind, 1680–1715*,
  introduction by Antony Grafton (New York: NYRB, 2013) [first
  published in French, 1935].
Jonathan I. Israel, *Radical Enlightenment: Philosophy and the
  Making of Modernity, 1650–1750* (Oxford: Oxford University
  Press, 2001) [chapter 27 situates Voltaire's contribution to the
  spread of English ideas in France].

Jonathan I. Israel, *Enlightenment Contested: Philosophy, Modernity, and the Emancipation of Man, 1670–1752* (Oxford: Oxford University Press, 2006) [chapter 29 discusses 'Voltaire's Enlightenment'].

Antoine Lilti, *The World of the Salons: Sociability and Worldliness in Eighteenth-Century Paris* (New York: Oxford University Press, 2015).

Larry F. Norman, *The Shock of the Ancient: Literature and History in Early Modern France* (Chicago: University of Chicago Press, 2011).

Karen O'Brien, *Narratives of Enlightenment: Cosmopolitan History from Voltaire to Gibbon* (Cambridge: Cambridge University Press, 1997).

Anthony Pagden, *The Enlightenment and Why it Still Matters* (Oxford: Oxford University Press, 2013).

John Robertson, *The Enlightenment: A Very Short Introduction* (Oxford: Oxford University Press, 2015).

Daniel Roche, *France in the Enlightenment*, trans. Arthur Goldhammer (Cambridge, Mass.: Harvard University Press, 1998).

J. B. Shank, *The Newton Wars and the Beginning of the French Enlightenment* (Chicago: University of Chicago Press, 2008).

J. S. Spink, *French Free-Thought from Gassendi to Voltaire* (London: Athlone Press, 1960).

Charles Withers, *Placing the Enlightenment: Thinking Geographically about the Age of Reason* (Chicago: University of Chicago Press, 2007).

David Wootton, *The Invention of Science: A New History of the Scientific Revolution* (London: Allen Lane, 2015).

On Voltaire

W. H. Barber, *Voltaire: Candide* (London: Edward Arnold, 1960).

W. H. Barber, 'Voltaire at Cirey: Art and Thought', in J. H. Fox, M. H. Waddicor, and D. A. Watts (eds), *Studies in Eighteenth-Century French Literature Presented to Robert Niklaus* (Exeter: University of Exeter Press, 1975), pp. 1–13.

David D. Bien, *The Calas Affair* (Princeton: Princeton University Press, 1960).

Stephen Bird, *Reinventing Voltaire: The Politics of Commemoration in Nineteenth-Century France* (Oxford: Voltaire Foundation, 2000).

J. H. Brumfitt, *Voltaire Historian* (Oxford: Oxford University Press, 1958).

Nicholas Cronk, 'Voltaire, Lucian, and the Philosophical Traveller', in
J. Renwick (ed.), *L'Invitation au voyage: Studies in Honour of
Peter France* (Oxford: Voltaire Foundation, 2000), pp. 75–84.

Nicholas Cronk (ed.), *The Cambridge Companion to Voltaire*
(Cambridge: Cambridge University Press, 2009).

Nicholas Cronk, 'Voltaire and the Posture of Anonymity', *Modern
Language Notes*, 126 (2011), pp. 768–84.

Nicholas Cronk, 'The Selfless Author: Voltaire's Apocrypha', *Romanic
Review*, 103 (2012), pp. 553–77.

Simon Davies, 'Voltaire's *Candide* as a Global Text: War, Slavery, and
Leadership', in Shaun Regan (ed.), *Reading 1759: Literary Culture
in Mid-Eighteenth-Century Britain and France* (Lewisburg:
Bucknell University Press, 2013), pp. 37–54.

Deirdre Dawson, *Voltaire's Correspondence: An Epistolary Novel*
(New York: Peter Lang, 1994).

André Delattre, 'Voltaire and the Ministers of Geneva', *Church
History*, 13 (1944), pp. 243–54.

Richard Fargher, 'The Retreat from Voltairianism, 1800–1815', in
W. Moore, R. Sutherland, and E. Starkie (eds), *The French Mind:
Studies in Honour of Gustave Rudler* (Oxford: Clarendon Press,
1952), pp. 220–37.

Pierre Force, 'Voltaire and the Necessity of Modern History', *Modern
Intellectual History*, 6 (2009), pp. 457–84.

Peter Gay, *Voltaire's Politics: The Poet as Realist*, 2nd edn (New Haven:
Yale University Press, 1988).

Russell Goulbourne, *Voltaire Comic Dramatist* (Oxford: Voltaire
Foundation, 2006).

John Gray, *Voltaire and Enlightenment* (London: Phoenix, 1998).

Diana Guiragossian, *Voltaire's 'Facéties'* (Geneva: Droz, 1963).

James Hanrahan, *Voltaire and the 'Parlements' of France* (Oxford:
Voltaire Foundation, 2009).

John R. Iverson, 'The Falsification of Voltaire's Letters and the Public
Persona of the Author: From the *Lettres secretes* (1765) to the
Commentaire historique (1776)', in E. Joe Johnson and Byron
R. Wells (eds), *An American Voltaire: Essays in Memory of
J. Patrick Lee* (Newcastle: Cambridge Scholars Publishing, 2009),
pp. 180–200.

John Leigh, *Voltaire: A Sense of History* (Oxford: Voltaire Foundation,
2004).

Margaret Sherwood Libby, *The Attitude of Voltaire to Magic and the
Sciences* (New York: AMS Press, 1966).

Haydn Mason, *Pierre Bayle and Voltaire* (Oxford: Oxford University Press, 1963).

Haydn Mason, *Candide: Optimism Demolished* (New York: Twayne, 1992).

Harvey Mitchell, *Voltaire's Jews and Modern Jewish Identity: Rethinking the Enlightenment* (London: Routledge, 2008).

John N. Pappas, *Voltaire and D'Alembert* (Bloomington: Indiana University Press, 1962).

Roger Pearson, *The Fables of Reason: A Study of Voltaire's 'contes philosophiques'* (Oxford: Oxford University Press, 1993).

Roger Pearson, 'White Magic: Voltaire and Galland's *Mille et une nuits*', in Philip F. Kennedy and Marina Warner (eds), *Scheherazade's Children: Global Encounters with the 'Arabian Nights'* (New York: New York University Press, 2013), pp. 127–42.

Síofra Pierse, *Voltaire Historiographer: Narrative Paradigms* (Oxford: Voltaire Foundation, 2008).

Síofra Pierse, 'Voltaire: Polemical Possibilities of History', in Sophie Bourgault and Robert Sparling (eds), *A Companion to Enlightenment Historiography* (Leiden: Brill, 2013), pp. 153–87.

Stéphane Pujol, 'Forms and Aims of Voltairean Scepticism', in S. Charles and P. J. Smith (eds), *Scepticism in the Eighteenth Century: Enlightenment, Lumières, Aufklärung* (Dordrecht: Springer, 2013), pp. 189–204.

R. S. Ridgway, *Voltaire and Sensibility* (Montreal: McGill-Queen's University Press, 1973).

Bertram Eugene Schwarzbach, *Voltaire's Old Testament Criticism* (Geneva: Droz, 1971).

Andrew Simoson, *Voltaire's Riddle: Micromégas and the Measure of All Things* (Washington, DC: Mathematical Association of America, 2010).

Samuel S. B. Taylor, 'Voltaire Letter-Writer', *Forum for Modern Language Studies*, 21 (1985), pp. 338–48.

William H. Trapnell, *Christ and his 'Associates' in Voltairian Polemic: An Assault on the Trinity and the Two Natures* (Saratoga, Calif.: Anma Libra, 1982).

Recordings

La Princesse de Navarre, Jean-Philippe Rameau (composer) and Voltaire (librettist): English Bach Festival Singers and Baroque

Orchestra, conductor Nicholas McGegan, 1980 (CD Erato, 0630-12986-2). Booklet notes by Lionel Sawkins.

Le Temple de la gloire, Jean-Philippe Rameau (composer) and Voltaire (librettist): Les Agrémens, Chœur de Chambre de Namur, conductor Guy Van Waas, 2015 (CD Ricercar, RIC 363). The first complete recording of the opera, using the revised 1746 version. Booklet notes by Julien Dubruque and Benoît Dratwicki.

Online resources

<http://voltaire.ox.ac.uk>
Gives details of the latest publications on Voltaire and links to the Voltaire Foundation blog.

<http://plato.stanford.edu>
The *Stanford Encyclopedia of Philosophy* (SEP) is an invaluable resource; it includes a fine article on Voltaire by J. B. Shank.

<http://artfl-project.uchicago.edu/tout-voltaire>
Tout Voltaire is a database containing all of Voltaire's writings (apart from his correspondence), freely available, in fully searchable form.

<http://www.e-enlightenment.com>
Electronic Enlightenment is a database containing extensive 18th-century correspondence, including the definitive collection of Voltaire's letters (available on subscription only, can be consulted in major research libraries).

<http://candide.nypl.org>
A fascinating online exhibition 'Voltaire's *Candide*' (2010) created by the New York Public Library.

Readers with knowledge of French may download the app 'Candide, l'édition enrichie', freely available on the Apple iStore, a joint production of the Bibliothèque nationale de France and the Voltaire Foundation in Oxford. This contains the full text in French, with a range of annotations and other resources to provide context; and it allows you to listen to the text, read by the French actor Denis Podalydès.

Publisher's acknowledgements

We are grateful for permission to include the following copyright material in this book.

Extract from Jorge Luis Borges and Osvaldo Ferrari, *Conversations, Volume 2*, trans. Tom Boll (London: Seagull Books, 2015).

Extract from George Bernard Shaw, *The Adventures of the Black Girl in her Search for God*, 1933, courtesy of The Society of Authors, on behalf of the Bernard Shaw Estate.

Richard Wilbur's 'Verses to Mme Du Châtelet', from *Mayflies: New Poems and Translations* by Richard Wilbur. Copyright © 2000 by Richard Wilbur. Reprinted by permission of Houghton Mifflin Harcourt Publishing Company. All rights reserved.

Ezra Pound's 'To Madame du Châtelet' in 'Impressions of François-Marie Arouet (de Voltaire)' (1915–16), by Ezra Pound, from *Personae*, copyright © 1926 by Ezra Pound. Reprinted by permission of New Directions Publishing Corp and Faber and Faber Ltd.

Extract by Ezra Pound, from *Selected Letters 1907–1941 of Ezra Pound*, copyright © 1950 by Ezra Pound. Reprinted by permission of New Directions Publishing Corp. and Faber and Faber Ltd.

Voltaire

Index

Voltaire

SOCIAL MEDIA
Very Short Introduction

Join our community
www.oup.com/vsi

- Join us online at the official Very Short Introductions **Facebook** page.
- Access the thoughts and musings of our authors with our online **blog**.
- Sign up for our monthly **e-newsletter** to receive information on all new titles publishing that month.
- Browse the full range of Very Short Introductions online.
- Read **extracts** from the Introductions for free.
- If you are a teacher or lecturer you can order inspection copies quickly and simply via our website.

ONLINE CATALOGUE
A Very Short Introduction

Our online catalogue is designed to make it easy to find your ideal Very Short Introduction. View the entire collection by subject area, watch author videos, read sample chapters, and download reading guides.

http://global.oup.com/uk/academic/general/vsi_list/

ENGLISH LITERATURE
A Very Short Introduction
Jonathan Bate

Sweeping across two millennia and every literary genre, acclaimed scholar and biographer Jonathan Bate provides a dazzling introduction to English Literature. The focus is wide, shifting from the birth of the novel and the brilliance of English comedy to the deep Englishness of landscape poetry and the ethnic diversity of Britain's Nobel literature laureates. It goes on to provide a more in-depth analysis, with close readings from an extraordinary scene in King Lear to a war poem by Carol Ann Duffy, and a series of striking examples of how literary texts change as they are transmitted from writer to reader.

{No reviews}

Free Speech
A Very Short Introduction
Nigel Warburton

'I disapprove of what you say, but I will defend to the death your right to say it' This slogan, attributed to Voltaire, is frequently quoted by defenders of free speech. Yet it is rare to find anyone prepared to defend all expression in every circumstance, especially if the views expressed incite violence. So where do the limits lie? What is the real value of free speech? Here, Nigel Warburton offers a concise guide to important questions facing modern society about the value and limits of free speech: Where should a civilized society draw the line? Should we be free to offend other people's religion? Are there good grounds for censoring pornography? Has the Internet changed everything? This Very Short Introduction is a thought-provoking, accessible, and up-to-date examination of the liberal assumption that free speech is worth preserving at any cost.

> 'The genius of Nigel Warburton's *Free Speech* lies not only in its extraordinary clarity and incisiveness. Just as important is the way Warburton addresses freedom of speech - and attempts to stifle it - as an issue for the 21st century. More than ever, we need this book.'
>
> **Denis Dutton, University of Canterbury, New Zealand**

GERMAN LITERATURE
A Very Short Introduction
Nicholas Boyle

German writers, from Luther and Goethe to Heine, Brecht,
and Günter Grass, have had a profound influence on the modern
world. This *Very Short Introduction* presents an engrossing tour
of the course of German literature from the late Middle Ages to
the present, focussing especially on the last 250 years.
Emphasizing the economic and religious context of many
masterpieces of German literature, it highlights how they can be
interpreted as responses to social and political changes within
an often violent and tragic history. The result is a new and clear
perspective which illuminates the power of German literature
and the German intellectual tradition, and its impact on the
wider cultural world.

> 'Boyle has a sure touch and an obvious authority...this is a
> balanced and lively introduction to German literature.'
>
> **Ben Hutchinson, TLS**

www.oup.com/vsi